Contents

3

About this book

Copyright is an important human right for artists of all kinds.

The visual artist is usually concerned with the making of an individual work, eg painting a picture, making a sculpture, and what happens to that one piece – the selling or exhibiting of it. Other uses, reproduction in newspapers or on postcards, and copyright concerns are often not considered.

This differs from other artforms such as literature, music, drama, where the artists and commissioners are selling or buying the right to use the original in some way – reproduce the manuscript or perform the choreography or musical notes – in effect, an act of copying. Because of this, those involved in such artforms are more likely to be aware of copyright issues.

It should be no different for visual artists however. Copyright is a concern for every piece of work – whether it is to be economically exploited by the artist, or to keep others from infringing the artist's right. Artists should ask themselves:

• Can I earn from copies of my work?

• Are copies of the work properly representing my art and me?

Copyright allows artists to exercise control over these issues as defined in the Copyright, Designs and Patents Act 1988 (referred to in the book as the copyright act). But the act, though defining the rights, cannot police them. The artist must do this by insisting on, and using, good practice and proper contracts.

This book emphasises the notion of good practice based on a sound understanding of copyright. It explains what copyright is, who owns it, how long it lasts, what can and can't be copied, and for what purposes copies may be made. It aims to help show how copyright can be used to earn money, through licensing, explaining the ideas of fees and royalties. Design right and patents can be used as well as copyright and all three are covered in the book.

For those who make, sell or copy work abroad there is information on the legal differences in countries which belong to the two main international copyright conventions.

It gives advice on how to judge whether your copyright or moral rights – a new area for British law – are being infringed, and what to do in those situations.

This book deals predominantly with the 1988 copyright act but the previous one of 1956 still applies to work made or commissioned before 1 August 1989 and, wherever relevant, the provisions of the 1956 act are made clear. The time differences between the acts and how to cope with them are dealt with by the 'transitional provisions' which attempt to bridge the gap.

The basic provisions of the copyright act are straightforward but the details are complex and often open to different interpretation. This book is a guide to the application of copyright for artists, craftspeople, photographers, designers, galleries, commissioners, agencies, etc to use in their everyday practice. It has been designed so the reader can use it as a constant reference book to help answer specific questions about copyright.

The book does not aim to give legal advice but to help give a general understanding of copyright and its application in particular cases. You should always use a solicitor or refer to one of the collecting societies to answer legal questions on a particular case.

1 • What is copyright?

Copyright protects an artist's exclusive right to reproduce or authorise others to reproduce the artist's work. The copyright act refers to all artists, writers, and composers and others by the title 'author'.

A work does not qualify for copyright until it has been 'fixed' in a medium, or form of expression. This means that an artwork is not subject to copyright until it appears on paper, or canvas, or is cast in bronze or some other medium. This is more of a problem for transient media such as performance than for other artforms. Live art is treated like dance and mime and must be recorded in written, video or other form to attract copyright or performance right protection.

see 'Design right', 10 • Designs, patents and Trade Marks
Original works of three dimensional design may also be protected by the new design right.

Moral rights, which are a new element in the 1988 copyright act, apply to the way in which a work is treated, and are intended to protect
see 9 • Moral rights
the artist's and the work's 'integrity', giving the artist the right to object to derogatory treatment of the work and to be acknowledged as the author of a work, or to have that acknowledgement withheld.

The concept of intellectual property

'A system of copyright law has two objectives: on the one hand, to associate the author with the economic exploitation of her/his work, and on the other hand, to preserve the intellectual relationship between the author and her/his work (moral rights).'

M. Wladimir Duchemin, Director of SPADEM, the French artists' collecting society, 1988

It is often difficult for people brought up under Anglo-Saxon legal systems (Britain, the USA) to grasp the concept of intellectual property. We are used to thinking of property simply as bricks and mortar, real estate, or the books, records, and works of art that we produce, or buy and sell. The concept of intellectual property, something that does not exist in solid form until it is fixed in a physically stable medium, perfectly fits the conventional process of making a work of art. The painting will exist only as a thought, or image in the artist's mind until put onto canvas, or some other medium that gives it a measure of permanence. The same is true of other forms of creative authorship. Music is a disembodied sound until it is fixed as notes on paper or sounds on magnetic tape.

The purpose of copyright is to protect the ownership of this intellectual property from unauthorised copying. One basic principle of copyright is the so-called 'idea-expression dichotomy'. The need for freedom to make ideas universally available is clear. There should be no monopoly on knowledge, access to which is a human right. But the actual expression of those ideas, or information, represents someone's work, and must be economically rewarded.

Copyright on a particular sculptor's work – for example a representation of the human figure in fibre glass – would not cover other representations of the human figure, only that original and exclusive work. In other words, copyright can protect an artist's actual artwork – the 'expression' – but does not prevent other artists from using the same process and dealing with the same subject matter – the 'idea' – provided always that they do not copy or adapt another artist's original work.

The idea-expression dichotomy

IDEA (PROCESS, SUBJECT)	EXPRESSION	COPY
Fibreglass sculpture	*Figure 1* by A. Sculptor	Photograph of sculpture for postcards
The Human Form		
Oil painting	*The Gulf* by A. Painter	Photograph of painting used in a magazine
War, The Gulf War		
Ceramic tiles	*Jungle* by A. Ceramicist	Adaptation of the leaf pattern into a textile design
Red & Blue Leaves		
▲ NO COPYRIGHT	▲ COPYRIGHT PROTECTION	▲ ONLY IF FAIR DEALING OR PERMITTED BY COPYRIGHT OWNER

"I'm Ali," said a boy. "At first I couldn't see anything because it was so dark, but then I saw the wolfman open a cupboard and evil looking green smoke came out and the clown was walking about on his hands with yellow lights flashing out of his shoes."

Helen Ganly, **Illustration from** *The Wolfman and the Clown*.
Helen Ganly wrote and illustrated this book published by Andre Deutsch. It was based on a real incident in Oxford where some children built a fantasy around a poster for the film *Restless Natives* by Ninian Dunnett which involved two characters dressing as a wolfman and a clown to pull a series of robberies. The poster asked – have you seen these characters – and the children thought they had. Helen Ganly developed a story from this totally unrelated to the film using imagery that was symbolic of contacts she had with dissident artists in Czechoslovakia (the clown's costume is the Czech flag, below the bookshelves is a portrait of Vaclav Havel).

Ninian Dunnett objected to the use of the characters, wanting acknowledgement on the cover of the book. Andre Deutsch agreed to put an acknowledgement slip in the book though they were under no obligation to do this. Ninian Dunnett's claim was on the idea of the wolfman and the clown. But there is no copyright in an idea only the expression of the idea. Helen Ganly's expression, her book, was totally different and unrelated to Ninian Dunnett's expression, the film.

Helen Ganly was later making a print from the clown drawing and noticed another artist using similar imagery. She realised that she was unconciously using an image common to twentieth century art of the clown dancing on his hands. Had she breached Picasso and Chagall's copyright? No, because she was not copying their work but sharing in the use of a common cultural symbol.

The principle of the idea-expression dichotomy holds good for all forms of original creative work. But visual artworks occupy a slightly different position in copyright from musical compositions, or dance, because the artwork is both the expression and the fixation of that expression in a medium. No work has legal existence in copyright until it is 'fixed' in a stable medium. A painting or sculpture does not have to be fixed or recorded after it has been made, because fixation occurs in the creative act. A live, or performed artwork, however, needs to be 'fixed' by recording in some way such as a video or a written description.

After fixation of a work, copies may be made (with permission), and the work commercially exploited. A painting though might remain a one-off and never be copied. It could be economically exploited by buying and selling, and be the only existing example. This weakens the economic power of the visual artist, because without copies in circulation to provide royalties and reproduction rights (as in the case of books, records, films), an artist may gain no further income from a work after it has been sold. Copyright confers the ability to control what happens to intellectual property – how it is used.

Artistic work

For the purposes of the copyright act, an 'artistic work' is defined as: any graphic work, (which includes painting, drawing, diagram, map, chart, plan, engraving, etching, lithograph, woodcut or similar work) sculpture; collage (which includes the re-use of images from other sources in an original creation); photographs produced by any method, including holography, a work of architecture being a building or model for a building, (all irrespective of artistic quality); and works of artistic craftsmanship (and here artistic quality is relevant).

What actually constitutes a 'work of artistic craftsmanship' is not defined in the act. There have been judicial rulings (before the present act came into force) that indicate anything designed with a purely functional purpose (in one case furniture, in another rainwear) and not with the intention of creating a work of art is not a work of artistic craftsmanship. The artist's intention seems to be the key. One test is 'is the work made by an artist-craftsperson?'

Meg Potter, **smoke fired porcelain vessels.** They represent an artist repeating similar forms and themes without reproducing a series of identical works. Since the 'main design' is being repeated the artist is not free to produce others in the series if copyright in one piece is assigned to the owner of that piece.

Originality

For an artistic work to qualify for copyright, it must be original. The definition of what is original seems to depend on the amount of skill, effort, creativity or work expended by the author on the artwork. One test of the degree of creative skill used has, in the past, been to identify the 'hand' of an individual artist at work. In one sense this is consistent with the principle of copyright protection, because anything that is simply a copy of an existing work would seem to be unoriginal, and therefore not qualify for copyright protection. But to be 'original' normally means no more than 'not copied'.

Artists often make a series of similar works on the same theme. These works are original and more works in the series can be made even if the artist doesn't own the copyright on the earlier works. The act says *'Where the author of an artistic work is not the copyright owner, he does not infringe the copyright by copying the work in making another artistic work, provided he does not repeat or imitate the 'main design' of the earlier work.'* But, if the artist is repeating the 'main design' of a work in which they no longer own the copyright, then the permission of the new copyright owner is needed. So beware of parting with copyright when making a series of work around the same theme.

2 • Who owns copyright?

Copyright normally belongs in the first place to the creator of an artwork, the artist – known in copyright law as 'the author'. The author may transfer ownership of the copyright to another person. Any fully effective transfer or assignment of copyright must be in writing, signed by the copyright owner.

see 5 • Licences & contracts

When an artwork is sold ownership of the copyright is not transferred unless there is a specific agreement to do that. Only the copyright owner can make such an agreement and they may not be the person selling the artwork. Always remember that physical ownership of an artwork – by purchase, loan or gift – does not include ownership of copyright.

Copyright comes automatically with the completion of an original artwork, which is known as the first ownership of the copyright. Ownership begins at the point when the work is 'made', recorded, or fixed in the stable medium of the expression.

There are exceptions to first ownership automatically going to the author of a work. In the case of an artist who produces work in the course of their employment, the employer is the first owner of copyright in the work. Other exceptions apply to Crown or Parliamentary copyright, and copyright vested in certain international organisations.

The author of certain artforms – sound recording, and films or videos – is the person who makes the arrangements for the work to be made, and so first ownership of copyright goes to that person; often in practice a producer or a company.

see 'Registered design', 10 • Designs, patents & trade marks

Ownership of design right is also automatic, it is not necessary to go through any formalities unless the artwork is to be registered as a Registered Design.

see 9 • Moral rights

The new moral rights arise automatically. These are subject to certain important exceptions.

If an artist is made bankrupt, the trustees in bankruptcy will automatically acquire the copyright in his or her works.

Qualifying persons

To be protected under the copyright act either the artist must be a 'qualifying person' at the time the work is made, or else the artwork must have first been 'published' in another country which is party to the Berne Convention or the Universal Copyright Convention.

A qualifying person is a British citizen, a British Dependent Territory citizen, a British national (overseas), a British Overseas citizen, a British subject or a British protected person under the Protected Persons Nationality Act 1981. People living in England, Wales, Scotland and Northern Ireland, who are not British citizens or nationals also qualify.

A work is published in another country when copies of it are issued to the public. This does not include exhibition of a work or the issuing to the public of copies of a graphic work (eg a drawing) or photographs of a sculpture or work of artistic craftsmanship.

see 12 • Copyright in other countries

Commissions & employment

Commissioned works are now, since the 1988 act, no exception to the rule that first ownership of copyright belongs to the artist, or author of the work, even if that work is commissioned. However in the case of 'design right' the commissioner owns the copyright, not the designer. For engravings, painted and drawn portraits, and photographs made *before* 1 August 1989 the commissioner owns the copyright.

see diagram 'Who is the first owner of copyright in artistic works', 13 • Copyright in brief

For the employed artist the position is very different: the act says that where an artistic work is created by an employee 'in the course of his/her employment', the *employer* is the first owner of the work, unless there is agreement to the contrary.

Employment means under a contract of service or apprenticeship. A 'contract *of* service' is usually full-time employment, as compared with freelance work under a 'contract *for* services', but there are many cases where this is difficult to determine. It will depend on factors such as: can the employer control the method or manner of the artist's work? Does the employee receive wages, as opposed to fees for hours put in? Is the artist entitled to paid holidays? Is he or she supplied with materials and equipment?

A contract of service need not be in writing, but even if it is in writing and the parties to the contract expressly say that their relationship is not one of employment this will not be conclusive if, when the above factors are considered, the artist is really operating as an employee.

However the act says that this rule will only apply *'unless there is agreement to the contrary'* which means that even where an artist is employed (or it is not certain whether he/she is or not) the artist can always agree with the other party that the artist will be the first owner of copyright, by including in the contract a simple clause to this effect. This is recommended in residencies or placements, and other cases where there may be doubt about whether an artist is employed or not.

Another example involves public art commissions, where the Inland Revenue has been targeting large commissions and insisting that the artists working on commissions are employees, with the result that PAYE must be deducted at source and the artist will be taxed under Schedule E (employees). Again a clause should be included in the commissions contract making copyright ownership clear, as well as moral rights. The ownership of moral rights is subject to the same distinction as above regarding employees and freelancers: if the artist has a contract of service, his/her employer will own the moral rights in the work, subject again to contrary agreement.

Parliamentary & Crown copyright

The Crown, or the Houses of Parliament, has first ownership of copyright in a work made by or on behalf of Her Majesty or Parliament.

Crown copyright applies to works made *'by an officer or servant of the Crown in the course of his duties '*. It lasts 125 years from the end of the year in which the work was first made. If the work is published commercially, less than 75 years from the end of the year in which it was first made, copyright lasts fifty years from the year of publication.

Parliamentary copyright covers works made *'by or under the direction or control of the Houses of Commons or the House of Lords'.* It lasts fifty years from the end of the year in which the work was first made.

The most obvious application of Parliamentary copyright is to the radio and television programmes broadcast from the Houses of Parliament, and to artists' sketches made of Parliament (photography is forbidden). This is material that might appeal to artists for use in their work, and the act appears to offer close control over it but that only covers works made under the direction or control of the House.

Keith Alexander, **tablecloth made as part of a workshop with Dunston Women's Craft Group during an artist-in-residence project funded by Gateshead Arts and Libraries. The tablecloth was made with the assistance of artist** Claire Satow.

This project is typical of the way Keith Alexander works. He ran workshops on design with Dunston Women's Craft Group. Claire Satow came in to introduce fabric printing skills. Members of the craft group designed and made the tablecloth. Keith Alexander's recent work has all been residency based and has used artists with skills he does not have. Whenever work is shown or reproduced all the participants are credited. Everyone involved in a project like this may want to use photographs of the work for different reasons. There should be a clear agreement saying what participants can make copies for and how the copy should be credited. This is totally different to the issue of who owns such a work.

Photo: © *Powerhouse Photography 1990*

see 'Commissions & employment' above

Joint authorship

'Joint authorship' of a work refers to a work produced by the collaboration of two or more artists in which the contributions of the authors are not distinct. Copyright is owned jointly by all the authors. Joint authorship is different from authorship of other sorts of collective works which may have been created by more than one author, each responsible for a separate part. A dramatic work, or a film, in which members of a team create separate, distinct elements, is a case in point. A work in which each author's contribution is distinct may be called a collective work, but it is not a work of joint authorship.

The term of copyright in a work of joint authorship lasts for the lifetime of the author living longest plus 50 years. Each one of a number of joint authors of a work may claim individual moral rights. There is no upper limit to the number of people who can be joint authors, but the work of each person should not be distinguishable from that of the other(s).

The question that arises if one artist invites another to help with a work has to be referred to the nature of the relationship between the two artists. Is one employing the other? If 'yes', the employer owns the copyright. Is one commissioning the other? If so, the second artist retains individual copyright over their distinct part of the work, if distinguishable. If the work of the two artists is not distinguishable they will be joint authors of the work. Each situation involves different copyright ownership, and

15

there should be a clear, written agreement to cover copyright, exercise of reproduction rights, credits and moral rights.

Unknown & pseudonymous authorship

Where the artist is not known, or cannot be found by reasonable enquiry (unknown authorship) or the work is published under another name (pseudonymous authorship) copyright still applies and lasts for fifty years after the work is first made available to the public. This will normally be the first time the work is exhibited in public. In the case of joint authorship this rule will only apply if none of the authors is known.

Proving ownership

Artists do not need to register or do anything to claim ownership of copyright in their own work – they own the copyright as a right, supported by the copyright act. Although it may be helpful to individual artists to compile lists – indexes – of works they have created, there is no legal requirement to do so in order to prove authorship. Such an index, backed perhaps by slides, photographs, or photocopies, could serve as a reference when checking copyright infringements or if ownership is in dispute. Membership of artists' rights societies does involve the keeping of indexes, which may be called on as evidence if it is necessary to prove ownership of copyright.

Another important reason to keep slides, photographs and videos of your work is that, even if you retain copyright when you sell the work, this is of no use if you can't get access to take photographs. Unless the buyer agreed to allow you access in a sale contract they are under no obligation to give you access to your work.

The use of the copyright symbol © to indicate ownership and date of creation or first publication of the work is recommended as a consciousness-raising measure, but it is not necessary in the UK, nor in see 12 • 'Copyright in other countries' countries adhering to the Berne Convention on Copyright. In countries which are party to the Universal Copyright Convention only, and which have copyright registration requirements (eg USSR) the symbol must be used together with the name of the copyright owner and date of creation or first publication. The use of the symbol is also recommended on all reproductions of work (eg postcards) – this should be insisted on in licence agreements.

Duration of ownership

The word 'term' is used in the copyright act to mean the duration of copyright. Artists' ownership of copyright in their original artistic work lasts for the artist's life plus 50 years from the end of the calendar year in which the artist died.

Copyright is part of an artist's estate. When an artist dies ownership passes to their heir(s). If you leave no will the laws of intestacy apply and certain relatives prescribed by law inherit your copyright. So it is better to have a will naming individuals to inherit your copyright, who you trust to exercise their judgement in ways you would have approved of in your lifetime. If you have a will but do not name special person(s) to inherit the copyright, it passes automatically to the person(s) inheriting the remainder of your personal property once specific bequests are dealt with. If no one is specified in a will to inherit moral rights, then the person who inherits the copyright will also inherit the moral rights. There are special rules for anonymous and pseudonymous works.

Ownership of copyright only passes from the artist to another person by agreement of the artist or the artist's heir(s). The term of copyright ownership is not affected by assignment or transfer. After expiry of copyright the work enters 'the public domain', when copying or reproduction are no longer restricted.

see 'Single European market', 12 • Copyright in other countries

Note that term of copyright is not, at the moment, uniform in different countries, although in many it is roughly similar. One of the effects of the Single European Market may be to unify copyright term.

Transferring ownership

First ownership of copyright by the artist means that, in principle, the artist may share in any economic exploitation of the work. This 'right to share' can be exercised by licensing the reproduction rights in a work to someone else. However copyright can be assigned (or transferred) by an artist in their lifetime. Assigning copyright ownership means actually handing it over to someone else. Licensing copyright means the artist remains the owner but permits reproductions etc to be made on certain conditions. In order for an assignment to be fully effective it has to be in writing, signed by the copyright owner.

The copyright act also allows 'partial assignments' where ownership is only transferred for a stated period less than the full copyright period (eg ten years) or where some, but not all, of the restricted acts of copying are being transferred. The distinction between an exclusive licence and a partial assignment is often technical and you should always seek advice about this.

An ownership problem

Under copyright law, there will not always be one level of copyright ownership generated from a single work of art. To illustrate: a sculptor completes a work – copyright ownership is automatic, and will last for the remainder of the sculptor's life plus 50 years.

The work is photographed, by a photographer commissioned by the sculptor, for obvious 'professional' reasons (documentation, proposals for potential exhibition or sale to galleries, etc). Now a second copyright exists, in the photograph of the sculpture, and that copyright is owned by the photographer. This second copyright doesn't extinguish the first, but exists alongside it.

What the photographer can do with the photograph depends on the agreement between themselves and the sculptor. For instance the photograph may be useable in advertising the sculptor's work, in an exhibition catalogue, in a specialist art magazine, in soliciting work, and in publicity for the sculptor, but for no other purposes. The sculptor may give permission for the photographic copy to be used for these purposes, and not, for example, sold by the photographer to a magazine for general use, or to an advertising agency. If there is no agreement covering these things sometimes one may be implied from the circumstances and purposes for which the photograph was taken but it is always preferable to have an agreement or exchange of letters making things clear.

If a news and general interest magazine decides to publish an illustrated article about the sculptor's work, a second photographer, employed by the magazine, may take a second photograph. Copyright in this second, magazine picture will belong to the magazine's publishers, if they employ the photographer.

At this point three copyright works exist – the original sculpture, and two different photographs, and three copyright ownerships exist.

We could assume that the sculptor has fairly effective control over what is done with the first photographer's picture, because it was commissioned for specific purposes, and the sculptor must have chosen the person who carried out the work. This commissioned photographer still owns copyright in the work, but is bound by an agreement with the sculptor based on the first copyright in the sculpture as to how the image

– the two-dimensional copy of the sculpture – may be used. Alternatively the photographer might be asked to assign the copyright.

The second, magazine photograph, is a different matter. The sculptor may have to deal with a large business enterprise, possibly an international corporation that owns magazines, newspapers, TV companies, advertising agencies, worldwide. The second photograph is in their picture library, copyright owned by the publishing company, it is available for many other possible uses, as illustrative material in a TV programme and accompanying book on contemporary art, for example. Unless the sculptor has been able to negotiate a specific licensing agreement with the magazine publishers, not much can be done to control the further use of the photographic copy of the sculpture. Moral rights could empower the sculptor to insist on being credited as the author of the sculpture, or object to derogatory treatment of the sculpture. Other questions arise: what about payment to the sculptor for further use of the (photograph of) the work, especially if it is issued worldwide? What about a jokey advert using the sculpture, or a version of it copied from the photograph?

see 'Right of authorship', 9 • Moral rights

This complex network of copyright ownership is not untypical, and can obviously become more complex as time passes, and the original artwork changes hands.

Monitoring copyright

Copyright ownership is crucial to controlling the use and economic exploitation of your artworks but one problem an artist faces, especially if they produce a lot of work, is tracking down all the potential or actual infringements of copyright. It is increasingly evident that modern technology makes copying simpler. Keeping hold of negatives no longer ensures that photographs cannot be reproduced. Computerised reprographic processes enable high quality copies to be made from a photograph printed in a newspaper. If artworks travel from one country to another then tracking down infringements becomes more complex. A practical and cost effective way of controlling this is to place the monitoring activity in the hands of a collecting society or agency.

see 'Blanket licences', 5 • Licences & contracts

3 • Artforms copyright applies to

Artists' books

Books made by artists range from traditional format (illustrated books with or without text) to one-off artworks.

An artist's book that is in effect an edition of prints bound into a folio will have copyright protection for each print as a separate graphic work.

An artist's book which is a single original artwork in book form may come under the definition of 'sculpture' or 'work of artistic craftsmanship'.

Literary works are, in copyright law, *'any work, other than a dramatic or musical work, which is written, spoken or sung'.* 'Writing' is not confined to the conventional processes of manual inscription or mechanical and electronic typing. The act defines writing as *'any form of notation or code, whether by hand or otherwise and regardless of the method... or the medium in or on which it is recorded'.* The written text of an artist's book, whether hand-drawn or written, or printed in some way, would be regarded as a literary work for copyright purposes. But the artistic work in it – eg drawings, diagrams, maps, charts, prints – would be regarded as separate artistic works.

Copyright in the typographical arrangement of a published edition belongs to the publisher and expires 25 years from the end of the calendar year in which the edition was first published. This means that publishers can often sue for copyright infringement in cases of unauthorised copying even though the copyright period of the literary work itself has expired.

Billboards

See under 'Murals' below.

Calligraphy

Original calligraphic works could be treated as drawings or paintings or possibly works of artistic craftsmanship. This will make an important difference if the work is sited in public *(see 'Crafts' below)*. In either case the artist will own copyright on the style and arrangement of the letterforms but not the text (ie the words and sentences) unless the artist were also the writer. Then the artist would own another copyright in the written text itself. Copyright will last for the artist's life plus 50 years. If calligraphy is used to produce a written, published work it could be treated as a typographical arrangement. A separate copyright would then belong to the publisher and last for 25 years from the date of publication.*See 'typographic arrangements' below.*

Cartoons

In general all original cartoons will qualify for copyright protection as drawings. There are additional possibilities for the protection of characters used in cartoons. If successful commercial exploitation is a real possibility, and every published cartoon has that potential, then 'character merchandising' may be relevant. This is the class of trade in which a character created for a fictional form – usually TV, film, cartoon or live drama – is used to market goods, for instance lollipops, watches, T-shirts. The best known examples, such as Disney characters, are exploited exhaustively (but only by the copyright owners or with their permission) as trade marks, actual 'live' impersonations in a range of contexts, and in three-dimensional copies of their flat originals. Copyright protection would enable the artist to prevent the unauthorised making of three-dimensional objects based on the original two-dimensional cartoons.

see 'Trade Marks', 10 • Designs, patents & trade marks

For the cartoonist, as well as copyright protection of the original artworks – which is a substantial safeguard – there are possibilities of using trade mark protection, the law against passing off or even design right if an industrial process is involved for the manufacture of the object derived from the cartoon representation.

An example of the use of copyright in character merchandising is 'Bananaman', a sort of fruity superhero, used on advertising material to sell bananas. Every example of the Bananaman image carries the by-line '© *D.C. Thomson Ltd*', identifying the publishers of the comic in which he originally appeared as copyright owners.

See also 'Illustration' below

Ceramics

see 10 • Designs, patents & trademarks

Studio ceramics could be treated as either sculpture or work of artistic craftsmanship. In either case the artist is the first owner of copyright in the work. If the ceramicist makes or authorises large numbers of a teapot, for example, then design right or registered design right could apply to protect it. *See 'Crafts' and 'Design' below.*

Collage

Collage is specifically listed as one of the types of artistic work protected by the 1988 copyright act. It was not in the 1956 act, which means that if the work was completed *before* 1 August 1989 it probably does not have copyright protection. If it was completed *after* 1 August 1989 it does

Paul Scott, *Free Mandela Collage No 5,* 1988, detail. Stoneware ceramic collage bowl. Though a ceramic 'bowl', this could, for copyright purposes, now be treated as a 'collage' or a work of 'artistic craftsmanship'. Collage is an important element in Paul Scott's work. *'I frequently use images and text in my work. Although often my own, I also make use of printed images and text. Where practical, I check the source for permission. I always acknowledge sources – either in the work itself, or by a written piece that goes with it. Artists should be able to use images and text freely without fear of legal or financial reprisals providing that they do so without exploiting the original artist or writer. Artists should always acknowledge their sources.'* Photo: *Andrew Morris*

have copyright protection.

As long as the restriction not to copy the whole or a substantial part of an original is observed, it seems that artists making collages may take bits and pieces from any source.

The key words in the copyright act are *'the whole or a substantial part of'* a work may not be copied. This is not always a question of physical measurement – 'substantial part' can mean 'key' or 'essential' feature. The use of visual 'quotations', or fragments of other works included as references, is acceptable in copyright law, provided the amount used is not a substantial part of the original. Collages of an artist's own previous work will not breach copyright, unless ownership of copyright has been assigned to another person. The questions arising from the use in an original artistic work, such as a collage, of images from other, possibly copyright sources, are complex and individual advice may be required. But creation of the collage establishes a copyright in it as a new work

see 8 • Permitted acts

If a collage is made from 'real' objects then the notion of copying does not apply. But if the collage was copied and made into a postcard then there could be infringement if the 'real' objects were themselves copyright works.

Action Space Mobile, *French's Hardware Shop, Still a Family Business.* This illustration is from, *The Eckington File,* a book that Mary Turner and Lee Sass of Action Space made during a community residency at Eckington. Copyright in the typographical arrangement of the book, since it is made and published by Action Space, belongs to the company. Copyright in photographs and writing belongs to the photographers and writers. But production of a community project involving a number of people makes ownership of copyright a complex issue. Action Space have clear guide-lines on this – whenever artists work with them their contracts assign copyright to the company. Their work involves books, films, puppet-making, murals, carnivals, performance, music, banners, theatre, cabaret, fireworks... often combined on the same project.
Photo: Mary Turner

Other related forms, such as video or film compilations or montages – which are not artistic works – are dealt with under the relevant artforms in this section.

Community art

This is a difficult category to place within copyright legislation, because the philosophy behind community art often includes the notion of a 'public domain' or public ownership. Community artworks could be said to belong to the community that has helped produce them.

Community art in the UK is quite a broad practice with the narrowest definitions favouring no individual authorship. Other interpretations are based on an artist working 'in' or 'with' a community to produce a joint or collective work. A community association or similar body employing an artist to work under a contract of service on a project would themselves own the copyright. But an artist commissioned to produce a community work could claim individual copyright ownership. If various artists have worked on a project and their contributions are not distinct, they will be joint authors unless they agree otherwise. They could agree to assign copyright to the organisation concerned.

The decision whether to assert moral rights of authorship in a community artwork and/or to pursue infringement of copyright will depend on each particular situation. On the face of it, an individual artist would not be morally justified in claiming sole copyright ownership for a collective work. Nor would it be fair for a community artwork to be exploited by commercial interests unconnected with the local community. However in law, and in the marketplace, 'fairness' and 'morality' may not always triumph.

Computer works

Until the 1985 copyright act, there was no provision for computer works in copyright. The Copyright (Computer Software) Amendment Act 1985 updated legislation, and this has now been replaced by the current, 1988 act. The 1985 act covers the period immediately before the 1 August 1989, when the 1988 act came into force.

Ron Haselden, *Windsweep,* 1990. A lightwork at Mount Edgecombe Country Park sequenced by the speed of the wind. Electronics by Mike Miller.
Here there are two elements – the 'sculptural' and the 'electronic'. The copyright on each is separate. Where a computer program is used in such a work it would be considered a computer-generated work as the program would control the work's function rather than be a tool in the making of the work itself, as with a computer-aided work.

A computer program is included in the copyright act as a species of literary work. No design right protection is available. In terms of copyright ownership in a program there is an important distinction between computer-aided and computer-generated works.

Computer-aided means that the work is created by the author, using a computer in the same way that a camera or other piece of equipment is used. The author/artist is the human operator of a technical aid, and the work produced is treated in the same way as any other artistic work created with the assistance of a tool. An example of this would be a work produced by an artist using a paintbox-type program. The copyright owner of such a work is the computer operator – ie the artist.

A computer-generated work is one that has been generated by a computer – ie without any human skill or effort in the resulting work. In these cases the copyright owner is *'the person who makes the arrangements necessary for the work to be created'*.

An example is the light tower on the roof of the Hayward Gallery by Roger Dainton and Philip Vaughan (1972/3). This is a sculpture made of neon tubes, the copyright in the configuration of which is owned by the artists. But that is only part of the artwork. There are also colour sequences produced by a program which changes with the weather the wind, temperature, etc. Since these can be said to be computer generated, copyright in the coloured sequences (the output) belongs to the person who made the arrangements for the creation of the work (probably the artists rather than the authors of the original program).

Copyright protection covers source code (written usually by programmer(s) employed by the company marketing the program) and the object or machine code, which is the result of the translation of the source code by the compiler or interpreter. The output is the result of interaction between program and data input.

UK copyright law does not, yet, offer much help with distinctions between the various stages in programming for computer art. The act's definition of 'translation' refers specifically to computer programs. Any shift of a computer program into another computer language, or out of computer language entirely, is a translation or adaptation of the original work, and is restricted by copyright. It would be just the same as adapting a two-dimensional artwork into a three-dimensional one.

When you buy commercially available packaged software, for example one that produces a design with a choice of methods, you pay for the right to use it (including the transition copying that takes place when the program is activated) but the copying of a substantial part (by volume) or any essential part, will be an infringement of the program's copyright

A computer program (including a computer-aided work) is treated as literary work and so copyright lasts for the author's life plus 50 years. In a computer-generated work copyright lasts for 50 years after the work was made.

Neither computer programs nor computer-generated works are protected by the moral rights of the artist to be identified as the author of the work or to object to derogatory treatment of the work.

Conceptual art

The original definition of conceptual art in the 60s was art which has not been put into a material form, but remains an unrealised idea, in the artist's head. However most conceptual art of that era did have a fixed form of expression. Yoko Ono, for example, issued a series of instructions – *thought-pieces* – in book form (which itself would attract copyright protection) for actions which were intended as live 'performances'. Dick Higgins produced word/performance pieces: *'The First Swallow you meet next Spring – that is my first performance'* from *'Do It Yourself, 1961-62'*. This could be classified as a script for a dramatic work. Higgins, and others, also produced diagrams to be traced in dance and performance pieces. These could be classified as a form of notation for a dramatic or dance work. By writing down or notating the artwork it has been put into a 'fixed form' and so can be protected by copyright.

Recently, the term 'conceptual' has been used to refer to time-based and transient 'live' art. Anything, in fact, that does not come within the description of plastic art in a stable medium. By definition, this work may only be afforded copyright protection if it is recorded, ie fixed, in some way. The Bulgarian/American artist Christo (Christo Javacheff) finances his time-based and transitory site-specific public artworks by selling drawings, prints, posters and postcards of the work. Drawings of Christo's projects are the copyright of the artist and exist as individual artistic works which in some cases, show unrealised works – they are not records.

Crafts

There is no definition in copyright law of 'crafts' but 'works of artistic craftsmanship' are included in the act as one of the categories of 'artistic work'. In defining artistic craftsmanship, the act takes a slightly different line from that used in defining other artistic works. The quality of the art is normally irrelevant to the copyright status of an artistic work. But for a work of artistic craftsmanship to qualify for copyright protection, it must have some discernible artistic quality. The usual distinction made by the courts is between an article made with the intention of creating a work of art and something made with the intention of creating a practical, utilitarian object. If the intention is to make a work of art or craft then the article is a 'work of artistic craftsmanship'.

Another key question is whether or not the craftwork is to be reproduced (ie copied) commercially. If so, the article may come within design right protection. It should be remembered that design right only applies to works made after 31 July 1989. In some cases craft items may be registered under the Registered Designs Act 1949.

see 'Design right'
10 • Designs, patents
& trademarks

If a work of artistic craftsmanship is permanently sited in a public place, copyright is not infringed if it is drawn, painted, photographed, filmed, or shown on television.

Design

Many media that would be called 'design' by artists, craftspeople or designers will be treated as a works of artistic craftsmanship or other artistic works – for instance textile design, graphic design or architectural design. These would all be subject to copyright protection. But designs can also be protected by unregistered or registered design right. A design may start out as an artistic work, and be protected by copyright, but subsequently become subject to design right. For example an original one-off wooden container (work of artistic craftsmanship) that is then put into mass production as a commercially exploitable product (item of packaging).

see 'Design right'
10 • Designs, patents
& trademarks

Drawing

Drawings come under the umbrella term 'graphic works'.

Drawings often have another function, apart from that of original works of art, they may also be the evidence of the authorship of a later (often three-dimensional) work.

Drawings may also be embodiments of the design that will at some later stage be economically exploited. Drawings in this category may qualify for design right, because they are 'design documents' but in

see 'Design right',
10 • Designs, patents
and trade marks
this case copyright protection will no longer be available to prevent articles being copied commercially.

Architectural drawings have a special status. They may be seen as a graphic representation of the work of architecture in question not design documents. Drawings made of buildings permanently situated in public are not a breach of copyright, and may be issued to the public, for example by being shown on television. The copyright in the original architectural drawings belongs to the architect. The copyright in the drawing made of a finished building, belongs to the author of that drawing.

An architect may be expected to hand over the actual drawings to the owner of a building but this does not mean that copyright on the building design has been transferred.

Engraving

Engravings are specifically included in the copyright act in the definition of 'graphic work'. The 1956 copyright act distinguished between artworks such as prints and those that could be treated as photographs. This was see 'Commissions & employment', 2 • Who owns copyright? especially relevant to commissioned work, which belonged to the commissioner if a photograph, but to the artist if not – with the new act this distinction disappears.

The UK copyright act does not deal with the editioning of prints. The US Visual Artists Rights Act 1990 states that to qualify as a work of art, an edition of prints must be signed and consecutively numbered in an edition of 200 copies or less. The intention is to protect the artist and the public from unauthorised pirating of prints. Although no such limitation exists in the UK copyright act, it is in the artist's interest to observe professional scruples when dealing with print editions. Individual numbering and signing, with an indication of the total number of prints in the run is essential, ie $3/30$.

Fax or facsimile

For copyright purposes this is treated as a form of photocopying. *See 'Photocopying' below.*

Film

The copyright act defines film as *'a recording on any medium from which a moving image may by any means be produced'*. Video-tape, videodiscs, and videograms in any form yet to be developed are covered by this definition as well as film on celluloid. One of the changes brought about in the 1988 act is the separation of the sound track from the film. The sound recording on a film was treated as part of the film in the 1956 act, but it is now dealt with as a separate work for copyright purposes, and is like other sound recordings.

The owner of the copyright in a film is defined in the act as *'the person by whom the arrangements necessary for the making of the film are undertaken'*. This is most likely to be the producer, or the company responsible for producing the film. Directors of films do not automatically own copyright in their films, but they may assert moral rights.

Copyright in a film or video lasts for fifty years after it was made or released. Releasing a film means a public showing, a television broadcast or cable networking.

Films are usually combinations of different artforms – written script, acted performance, music, and design or artwork, all of which have separate copyright protection and ownership. The owner of an existing copyright in a work used in, but not created specially for, a film must be consulted to obtain permission for use. The act contains a specific exception in the case of buildings, sculptures, and works of artistic craftsmanship, if permanently sited in a public place or in premises open to the public on public display. Also there is a further exception – if an artwork is included 'incidentally' in a film or TV broadcast this will not be breach of copyright in the artwork.

There is no copyright protection on a photograph made from a single frame of film – it is neither photograph nor film!

Folklore

There is no protection for artistic works of folk art, in the UK. The copyright act does contain a provision for the recognition of bodies set up in other member countries of the EC or the Berne Convention that have the power to enforce copyright in works of unknown authorship, if it can be shown that the author was an inhabitant of or lived in that country. In other words, works that were created anonymously, and have become part of a country's heritage may be protected under copyright, and this protection will be recognised throughout the 'convention countries'. This measure is clearly intended to protect national heritage against commercial exploitation, and it should be seen in the context of export control of items of folklore and national traditional culture. This is of particular relevance to galleries that deal in folk art from other countries.

Glass

Studio glass and stained glass could be treated as either works of artistic craftsmanship or other artistic works. In either case the artist is the first *see 'Definition of* owner the copyright but there are important differences if the work is *artistic work',* publicly sited *(see 'Crafts' above and 'Public Art' below)*. If the artist makes *1 • Who owns* large numbers of an article then registered or unregistered design right *copyright* could be applied to it. *See 'Design' above.*

Graphic design

Original works of graphic design would be treated as drawings or *see 'Design right',* paintings. A design that is used on a manufactured article (say a transfer *10 • Design, patents* for a range of ceramics) cannot be protected by the new design right but *& trade marks* may be protectable by registered design.

Illustration

There is nothing exclusive to illustration that is not covered in the copyright act by the various techniques employed by illustrators; eg drawing, engraving, printmaking, etc. The Association of Illustrators (AOI) published a short guide by Simon Stern to the 1988 copyright act for its members in 1989: *Rights – the illustrators guide to professional practice.* According to this, advertising agencies' fear that the new moral right to object to derogatory treatment of a work would hinder practices like cropping and over-printing have been unfounded. Only unreasonable treatment is likely to cause problems. The AOI also feels the illustrator/ artist's right to be credited with authorship has not caused the problems that some users anticipated. The AOI recommends that illustrators deal with the issue of acknowledging authorship by *'an ordinary contractual agreement about credits',* instead of either asserting or waiving that moral right. This may seem a compromise that weakens the principle of moral rights but it is probably the best solution for illustrators in the short term.

Allan Francis, *The Golden Age of Empire,* site-specific installation. Part of Project UK's 'New Work Newcastle '89'. The different elements of an installation are treated separately for copyright purposes as sculpture, photography, sound, etc. With a site-specific installation it is often the copyright status of the documentation that is most important, as this is the only 'permanent' result. The illustration includes a hologram which is treated as a photograph under the 1988 copyright act.
*Photo: Jon Bewley, © **Projects UK 1989***

An important point for illustrators is that where their work is published *'in a newspaper, magazine or similar periodical, or an encyclopaedia, dictionary, yearbook or other collective work of reference'* they have no right to be credited as the artist. The AOI feels that *'this leaves illustrators in the curious position that the Act gives the right to a credit in advertising work, provided it is asserted, but not in editorial work, a reversal of the previous custom. It should, however, be emphasised that the act does not prevent illustrators and writers being credited in editorial work; it merely refrains from making such credits a statutory right. Illustrators should therefore require a credit in editorial work as before.'*

The copyright in illustrations in a book will automatically be owned by the illustrator unless otherwise agreed or the production of the work was carried out under the illustrator's contract of service.

See also 'Cartoons' above.

Installation

This is a type of artwork that should be treated in terms of its constituent parts. Individual copyright will apply to those elements identifiable as

31

'paintings', 'sculpture', 'film', 'sound recording' and so on. There is no provision in the act for copyright protection for an installation as such.

Mail art

see 7 • Infringments of copyright

Mail art involves the free use of images by different artists, circulated by post throughout the world, so seems to be an artform in which copyright protection is neither demanded nor welcomed. To assume the right to copy and circulate other artists' work without permission is, of course, not normally advisable as it would be a breach of copyright. However by participating in mail art artists could be said, because of the customs of mail art, to be giving an implied licence for others to do things with the work which would otherwise be breaches of copyright. In the 60s there was a philosophy of 'Copywrong' and in recent years notions of sanctioned plagiarism have achieved currency amongst some artists. Whilst not wishing to encourage anyone to weaken the system of copyright protection which is so essential to the fair operation of a world art market, if artists wish to opt out of the copyright system, that is their concern. But it should also be noted that mail art does not, of itself, necessarily involve either plagiarism or abandoning the copyright system.

Murals & billboards

A mural will normally be a 'graphic work' for copyright purposes. However a mural made from mosaic or brickwork, or a ceramic, stone, metal or wooden relief panel or any mural that might be described as a work of artistic craftsmanship or sculpture, may be drawn, painted, photographed, filmed, or shown on television, without infringement of the copyright, if the mural is permanently situated in a public place, or in premises open to the public. Copies of the work may be made and issued to the public, including the broadcast of television images of the work, without infringing copyright.

In spite of the lack of protection against copying by photographing or otherwise of a work *permanently situated in public',* the artist who creates a public mural does have the moral right, to be identified as the author (if this right has been asserted), whenever a graphic or photographic copy of the work is issued in public.

See 'Public art' below.

The Changing Picture of Docklands, Peter Dunn and Lorraine Leeson **of Docklands Community Poster Project. These 18' x 12' photomurals were shown on six billboard sites in London's docklands 1982-84. They were made from photomontage with acrylic glazes onto board. They were changed over a period so the whole image gradually evolved. Although sited in public the billboards are clearly temporary and are neither sculptures or works of artistic craftsmanship and therefor permission is needed to copy them.**

Painting

A painting is defined as a graphic work, and treated in the same way as a drawing, engraving, etching, lithography, etc.

Under the 1956 copyright act, portraiture was treated differently from other forms of painting. The commissioner of a portrait became the copyright owner. This is no longer the case. Some of the considerations that apply to collage may apply to a painting in so far as it involves use of imagery from other people's work.

Parody

The underlying basis of parody, satire, etc is to take an existing work, and alter it so creating a new work that is a humorous version of either the original work or the style of the original author. Sally Swain's book *Great Housewives of Art* is a good example of parody in art, which appears to have used famous artworks – some by living artists – without infringing copyright. The copyright in the book is credited to Sally Swain.

There is no specific permission given by the copyright act for parody and satire to be exempted from the basic rules of copyright; however parody which uses an idea from an existing copyright work, but also uses substantial skill and labour of its own, will probably not infringe copyright in the original.

Performance

The treatment of performance or live art as a 'dramatic work' seems to be the logical solution to achieving copyright protection for this artform. It is only possible to claim copyright on a dramatic work once it has been fixed in a stable medium. It is suggested that for performance, fixation should be in either written or diagrammatic form – a dramatic script or a choreographic notation. A written version of a performance would also

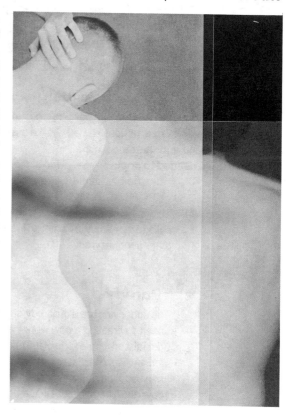

Louise Tonkin, *Fuschia.* *Fuschia* is a fifty minute show combining dance, performance, slides, text and sound (sound collage and saxophone by Lol Coxhill). Of itself this photograph would not be sufficient to 'fix' the performance and qualify it for copyright or performance right. More photographs, written description, sound recordings, dance notation, etc would be needed, though copyright would clearly apply to the slides and any recorded sounds. The photograph is used by Louise Tonkin for publicity. Copyright in the photograph belongs to Tansy Spinks who has used it in an exhibition. Both uses are obviously compatible and each artist benefits from the others' use of the image. *Photo: Tansy Spinks*

be regarded as a literary work for copyright purposes and a drawn version as a separate artistic work. Photography, film or video might also be used to record the actual performance, in which case separate copyright works and questions of copyright ownership would arise. *See Film, Photography and Video.*

Where the artist is not the creator of the record of the performance, there will be two copyright works owned by different people, one in the performance as a dramatic work and another in the photograph, film or video. Since, to be a protected dramatic work the performance must be fixed in tangible form, the record could be evidence of the performance in a 'fixed form', even if it is done without the performance artist's permission, and so be used by an artist to prove the existence of copyright or performance rights in their performance. But the record may not alone suffice to prove copyright ownership in the work (for example it may be a dance written by someone else). It may certainly be used to prove ownership of 'performance rights' which are slightly different from copyright. Part II of the 1988 act incorporated performance rights in live performances for the first time. Previously these had been covered by the Performers Protection Acts, the most recent of which was passed in 1972. Performers do not actually have copyright in their performances, but there is civil law right as well as the criminal law to protect against unauthorised recording or transmission of a performance, and commercial dealings in illicit records. Performance rights refer to dramatic and musical performances, readings, recitations and variety performances, *or any similar presentation'*. Many of the characteristics of performance rights are similar to those that apply to copyright.

A person with an exclusive recording contract also has rights under the act. An exclusive recording contract is the means by which the rights to record a performance are acquired by someone other than the performer. This licence excludes all others, including the performer, from making a recording of the performance for the purpose of commercial exploitation.

The duration of performance rights is 50 years from the year of first performance of the work, which is less than copyright. There seems no reason why a performance artist should not take advantage of both copyright and performance rights.

Photocopying

It was the introduction of widespread photocopying that led to much of the 1988 legislation. Reprography – large scale copying – has meant that protection of copyright material has become progressively more difficult. The 1956 Act did not deal with reprography adequately. Most of the problems that have arisen from photocopying concern literary or musical works. The advent of laser colour copying means artworks are now as easily reproducible as written texts and musical scores.

Helen Chadwick, *Of Mutability*, photocopy and assorted media, installation ICA, London 1986. Collection of the V & A Museum. The different elements of an installation are treated separately, each with its own copyright status. This shows 'sculpture' and 'photocopying'. As it was made before 1 August 1989, copyright on the 'sculpture' lasts for the artist's life plus 50 years, for the photocopies (treated as photographs) it is 50 years from date of first 'publication' (ie public showing). The duration of copyright on a photocopy made after 1 August 1989 is the artist's life plus 50 years.
Photo: Edward Woodman

An original work which was produced by means of a photocopier can still be an artistic work and attract copyright protection but not if it is merely a photocopy of another work.

Artists who wish to work with the photocopier as a tool should remember they may not copy other artists' work without permission, except under the terms of fair

see 8 • Permitted acts   dealing (eg research, private study, criticism or review), which exclude the making of copies for commercial exploitation, or unless the copying is not substantial.

The facsimile machine, or fax, and can be regarded for copyright purposes as a form of photocopier and the same considerations apply.

Photography

Photographs are now specifically included by the 1988 act as being within the definition of 'artistic works'. Under the 1956 act photographs were an exception, copyright ownership depending on who had supplied the film, or had commissioned the photograph. Under the new act, the photographer, even if commissioned (but not if employed) now owns the copyright. Duration of copyright is the same as for other artistic works, the life of the photographer plus 50 years. All the other provisions of copyright ownership in artistic works now apply to photographs. The definition of a photographer is the person who creates the photograph. The definition of photograph is *'a recording of light or any other radiation on any medium on which an image is produced or from which an image may by any means be produced, and which is not part of a film'*. This definition includes a hologram.

Photographers who exhibit work in galleries are now treated in the same way as other artists for the purposes of copyright. If the photographer's professional outlet is in newspaper and magazine publication, there are important exceptions in the case of moral rights, which also affects illustrators. These cover the right to be identified (credited) as the author: the right does not apply in the case of photographs made for the purpose of reporting current events or photographs used in newspapers, magazines or other periodicals or in reference books.

Because of the change in copyright regulations for photographs from 1 August 1989, anyone wishing to use photographic material should be acquainted with the different terms of copyright ownership. The diagram 'How long does copyright last?' in chapter 13 'Copyright in brief', helps explain the situation. Before the 1956 act (commencement 1 June 1957) the term of copyright ownership in photographs was 50 years from the year in which the photograph was taken. For photographs taken between 1 June 1957 and 31 July 1989, the term of copyright ownership was 50 years from the date of first publication. Any unpublished photographs taken in this period are protected for 50 years from the end of 1989.

see 'Rights of privacy', 10 • Moral rights

There is provision in the moral rights section of the 1988 act to protect the privacy of photographs and films commissioned for private and domestic purposes. These may not be shown in public in any way without permission from the commissioner. The intention is to protect photographs such as wedding pictures from misuse, particularly by the press.

Portraiture

Under the 1956 act, the commissioner of a portrait owned the copyright in any form, painting, photograph, etc. This is no longer so, the 1988 act has put portraiture in the same category as other artistic works.

Printmaking

Copyright remains with the artist who produced the original print, however many copies are made. Licences to others to create prints should always be limited by stipulating the number of prints, number of editions, and a time limit. This is a field in which economic exploitation of an original can be very wide, and extreme care is advised. *See under 'engraving', and 'illustration' above.*

Prints that were made by photographic methods were in an ambiguous position under the 1956 act, depending on whether they were considered to be like ordinary photographs or more like other artistic works, but that has now been clarified by the inclusion of photographs in the category of artistic works.

see diagram 'Who is the first copyright owner', 13 • Copyright in brief

Public art

As this is a description of a use of artworks, rather than a distinct artform (it encompasses, painting, sculpture, ceramics, crafts, etc) information will be found under specific headings. The copyright act distinguishes sculpture and works of artistic craftsmanship from all other types of artistic works on public display. This exception to general copyright provision applies to buildings, sculptures, models for buildings and works of artistic craftsmanship, which, if permanently situated in a public place or on premises open to the public, may be drawn, photographed, filmed, videoed, and the copies broadcast, or issued to the public, all without infringing copyright in the works. In other words, no permission is needed from the artist or copyright owner to make these 'copies' of a public art work, as long as it is permanently sited in public. The prohibition on photography that is seen in many public galleries may only be enforceable if there is a contract issued in the form of a ticket, between the gallery and the visitor.

Under the provisions on moral rights, provided the artist has properly asserted his/her right of authorship, then even if photographs, films, etc are made without permission, the artist must be credited when the photographs or film is shown.

In most cases artists should retain copyright in commissioned works and give the commissioner limited licence restricting the commissioner's use of reproductions of the work to promotional purposes.

Note that under the 1988 act, the new design right, which protects the commercial exploitation of certain designs, is automatically first owned by the commissioner, even though the copyright in the

Barbara Kruger, *We don't need another hero,* billboard. A sculpture or 'work of artistic craftsmanship' which is permanently sited in a public place can be drawn, painted, photographed, filmed or shown on television without infringement of copyright. Barbara Kruger's mural, although publicly sited would be treated as a 'graphic work' and such copying would be an infringement of copyright. But Barbara Kruger is unconcerned with copyright. She re-uses found imagery and is keen to have her work reproduced as much as possible. This billboard was commissioned by Artangel Trust for display in London and thirteen other cities concurrent with Channel 4's series 'State of the Art'. Artangel's policy on projects is that it retains the right to use documentation for publicity purposes but copyright of all artwork remains with the artist. *Photo:* John Carson

original work or drawings of the work will be owned by the artist. This odd situation can be avoided by including a clause in the contract which assigns the design right to the artist.

Sculpture

This is one of the classes of artistic work specifically designated in the copyright act. The same rules apply to copyright ownership of a sculpture as to all other artistic works. The exception made in the case of sculpture permanently situated in public is dealt with under 'public art'.

Sculpture, as defined in the act, includes a cast or model made for purposes of sculpture. The implications for copyright ownership are that each cast is a separate copyright work, even if reduced in size.

Some foundries and dealers operate an editioning system where twelve casts are made and numbered and one cast is made as an artist's copy. Similar systems operate under legal controls in other countries but in the UK this is merely an accepted practice. It has no legal status. Multiple versions of a sculpture may push the work into the area of design right.

Keith Piper, *Chanting Heads.* The sound track consisted of 'samplings' of song, chanting, poetry and oratory from various sources. No copyright clearance was sought. This was an Artangel project. Artists often create such sound-tracks appropriating sound and images from many sources without encountering problems. Artangel's policy is to retain the right to use project documentation for publicity purposes but copyright of all artwork remains with the artist.

Sound

Sound or recordings of sound may form part of an artist's installation, and also be used in sculpture and performance.

Sound recordings are treated as separate copyright properties when used, for instance, in film and video or in a tape-slide sequence. The copyright in a sound recording belongs in the first place to the person *'by whom the arrangements for making the recording... are undertaken'* and lasts for 50 years from the end of the calendar year in which it was made.

Sound recordings can also be protected under the provisions of performance right; *see 'performance'.* Note that the definition of a sound recording in the copyright act is divided into two parts:

• a recording of sounds, from which the sounds may be reproduced: this means things like natural sounds, bird song, or trains, gunfire, etc; and

• a recording of the whole or any part of a literary, dramatic or musical work from which sounds reproducing the work or part may be produced.

The important difference is that anyone may record bird song, but a particular, existing recording is subject to copyright restriction, and cannot be copied without permission. To record another work (of music, etc) requires permission of the copyright owner. The organisations that deal with licensing the playing of recorded music – Performing Rights Society, Mechanical Copyright Protection Society, and Phonograph Performance Ltd, are listed at the end of this book.

see 16 • Contacts

The provisions of fair dealing do not allow home taping or copying from disk onto cassette, except in the case of 'time shift' recording of television programmes (recording them to watch at another time in the home). However, if the taping of music is for private, domestic use, not commercial exploitation, it is not a criminal offence but a civil one. The widespread use of 'dubbing' tape machines, much opposed by the music industry, leads to frequent technical offences against copyright law. Only a levy on tapes or equipment would satisfy the recording industry, and Germany does have such regulations, but the British Government has decided against it.

Textiles

see 'Registered designs', 10 • Design, patents & trade marks

Textiles may be works of 'artistic craftsmanship'. Designs used on textiles will be 'graphic works'.

Design right protection will only be available for three-dimensional designs. *See 'Design' above.*

Theatre design

see 'Commissions & employment', 2 • Who owns copyright

Theatrical, film or television set design, like costume and property design, is an area of work that is covered by copyright provision for artistic works. The possibility of further use of a designer's work in a different context is important. A designer may create costumes or scenery for a play which is subsequently adapted for television or film, or work created for one production may be used in another production. The designer's contract should contain a licence defining how and where the theatre management is permitted to use the work.

see 5 • Licences & contracts

The case of lighting design is different, because, although any original drawing may be protected by copyright, and so copies of the design cannot be made without permission, the actual use of lighting designs in a production is not a restricted act and thus is not protected by copyright. There is no provision in law for performance right protection for a lighting design, because it is deemed to be an artistic work. So the licence for using the designs in the designer's contract needs to be carefully worded. A lighting design that is embodied in a computer program is protected by the same copyright provision that covers computer works. *See 'Computer Works' above.*

Typefaces

The design of typefaces will be protected as 'artistic works'. Naturally, typefaces may be used iVthe ordinary course of typing, composing text and printing, and the act specifically permits these uses. But commercial dealing in (making, selling, etc) a copyright typeface is an infringement of copyright.

Typographical arrangement

There is separate copyright in the actual typographical arrangements used in a publication. This means that although works out of copyright, for example Shakespeare's plays may be copied, a particular edition may not be copied if the typographical arrangements attracts and is still under copyright. The copyright of the typographical arrangement of a published edition belongs to the publisher and expires 25 years from the end of the calendar year in which the edition was first published.

Video

No distinction is made in copyright between video and film, and everything that applies to film applies to video. *See 'Film' above.*

4 • The uses of copyright

Exhibitions & sales

see 8 • Permitted acts

Sale of an artwork does not transfer ownership of copyright. However galleries, dealers and agents have the right to reproduce the artwork for the sole purpose of advertising the sale of that artwork; this new exception was introduced by the 1988 act. The exception does not apply to the advertising for sale of a *copy* of the artwork.

If you assert your moral rights then any exhibited work must identify you as the artist. You should assert your right of authorship by identifying yourself on the work, the mount or the frame. This assertion of authorship is binding on subsequent owners of the work *'whether or not the identification is still present or visible'*. All contracts, licences or agreements with galleries, exhibitors, dealers or private buyers should include a written assertion of the right of authorship and a statement making it clear that copyright has not been transferred as part of the sale.

see 'Right of authorship', 9 • Moral Rights

see 5 • Licences & contracts

If you have made any agreement allowing the exhibitor or new owner of the artwork to copy it in any way it should be made quite clear in writing (ie as part of the contract) what form the copying can take (eg catalogue or postcard), how many copies can be made (eg 500 posters, 1000 catalogues), what purpose it can be used for (eg to advertise an exhibition), how long the permission to copy lasts (eg duration of exhibition, two years, until first edition of catalogue is sold out), where the copies can be distributed (eg UK only) and what fee, if any, is payable. Any sale agreement should preferably also allow the artist access to the work to take photographs or to borrow it for exhibition.

see 6 • Fees & royalties

There is no legal requirement on those who deal in art, or who act as agents for artists or for collectors, to reveal the identities of purchasers of art but it is possible to ask galleries or dealers to do so in your contracts with them. It is only by monitoring breaches of copyright that an artist or an artist's society can keep track of the commercial exploitation of works. Infringements of moral rights must also be monitored. For the individual artist to keep track of work once it has been sold is extremely difficult. One solution to the problem of monitoring copyright and moral rights observance lies with artists' collecting societies. Collective action is provided for in the copyright act, although it is less developed in practice in the visual arts than in the fields of musical, dramatic and literary creation. Blanket licensing of words and music played in public places (either live or in recorded form, including broadcasting) enables the composers and performers to receive a return in proportion to the use made of their work.

Art in public spaces

The copyright act makes a distinction between sculpture and works of artistic craftsmanship on public display, and all other types of artistic works on public display. Buildings, sculptures, models for buildings and works of artistic craftsmanship, if permanently situated in a public place or in premises open to the public, may be drawn, photographed, filmed, videoed, and the copies broadcast, or included in a cable programme, or issued to the public, all without infringing copyright in the original works. In other words, no permission is needed from the artist or copyright owner to make these 'copies' of a 'public' art work. Even works in galleries that are 'open to the public' fall within this exemption. However, even where for this reason there is no breach of copyright, the prohibition on photography that is seen in many public galleries will be enforceable if there is a contract issued in the form of a ticket, between the gallery and the visitor.

Catalogues

The catalogue is an important part of exhibiting. Most exhibition contracts will include a provision for a catalogue, and the artist will be asked to permit reproductions of works to be made for inclusion. Though often in the artist's interest to comply it is important to remember that artwork can only be reproduced in a catalogue without the artist's permission if the artwork itself is being advertised for sale. Where copyright in a work is not owned by the artist, the copyright owner must be consulted. Usually permission to reproduce a copyright work will be sought in respect of use in the catalogue only, and nowhere else. If sales of a catalogue are planned after the exhibition, it is legitimate for the artist, or copyright owner, to ask for a licence that reflects this with payment, or for the exhibition contract to include this as a clause. A royalty should in effect be payable to the artist for use of works in what is actually a publication independent of the exhibition. The catalogue effectively becomes a book, and permission for the use of copyright work should reflect this.

Postcards & posters

A poster to advertise an exhibition can use a copy of a work in the exhibition without permission if it advertises the sale of the work itself but it cannot do this after the work is sold. An exhibition contract should specifically refer to such use of copies of works.

Galleries often make postcards of works on display or in their permanent collections. Even if a gallery owns an artwork, permission must be sought from the copyright owner before postcard copies of the work may be made. Remember, if the gallery is selling the cards rather than, or as well as, using them as invitations, they will be making an income from them and should pay a fee or royalty. Postcards could be given to the artist in lieu of fee and this is often a good way of sorting out payment on reproductions for invite cards.

see 'Checklist for non-exclusive licence', 5 • Licences & contracts

see 6 • Fees & royalties

Public art

In public art, as in all situations of employment or commission, artists and commissioners are strongly advised to make copyright provisions in their contracts. Artists should beware of commission contracts which contain a clause assigning copyright ownership to the commissioner. Artists should in most cases retain copyright in commissioned works of public art and give the commissioner a limited licence restricting the commissioner's use of reproductions of the work to promotional and non-commercial purposes. If a commissioner wants a more extensive licence, an artist should carefully consider if this is justified and whether a royalty or added commission fee should be charged. Similarly it is possible for an employer to contractually arrange that copyright in a work created by an employee is assigned to the employee.

see 'Commissions & employment', 2 • Who owns copyright

Public art that involves the creation of multiple copies of single works of craftsmanship – cast ironwork for street furniture, ceramic tiles, banners and flags, even original sculpture – might involve design right protection, especially if the artist is commissioned by a large enterprise to decorate a considerable area of property development. Under design right, where an artist is employed *or* commissioned to make a design work, the employer or commissioner is the original owner of the design right. Again a commission contract can assign copyright to the artist.

see 'Design right', 10 • Designs, patents & trade marks

A similar problem exists with residency and placement contracts. If the artist is employed then copyright ownership in the work produced by the artist during the residency will, unless contractual arrangements are used to say otherwise, belong to the employer. This is becoming an important issue now that the Inland Revenue are increasingly questioning self-employment arrangements between artists and agencies organising residencies. Again there should be a clause in the contract making it clear that the artist owns copyright

If a sculpture or work of artistic craftsmanship is permanently sited in a public place, copyright is *not* infringed if it is drawn, painted,

Kate Russell, *Signs of Life and Death,* woven textile construction. Kate Russell commissioned this photograph in 1986. The image is one of a set of sixteen postcards. She had 5000 of each printed and two full-colour A2 posters. The cost was £6000 which the printers, Lund Humphries, 'sponsored' by giving her extended credit. It took two years of selling to pay off the debt. The cards still provide around £100 a month income. Because the photograph was made before 1 August 1989 the copyright belongs to Kate Russell as commissioner. If she commissioned it now the copyright of the photographs would belong to the photographer unless otherwise agreed. Any agreement with the photographer should specify usage.

photographed, filmed, or shown on television. Care must be taken that this does not lead to an abuse of the rights of the copyright owner. Fortunately the moral right to have authorship acknowledged still applies to work sited in public, so there is some control. Moral rights do not, however, carry any economic implications. The possibility of using filmed or videoed public art as part of a television broadcast exists within the provisions of the act. There is

Anne Finlay, **earrings, polyester film and plastic coated wire.**
Anne Finlay's slide was on the Crafts Council's slide index. You
do not have to go into the Crafts Council to use their index, they
will send you slides. When you get them there are very clear
instructions as to how you can use them – *'slides may be
borrowed at a nominal charge for educational purposes... they
are available to journalists and publishers on a sliding fee
scale... permission must be sought for reproduction... slides
must not be copied... slides must not be projected for more than
sixty seconds at a time'.* Permission for reproduction is always
referred back to the maker. When you go on the Crafts Council's
slide index all this is made clear to you. Some slide indexes
don't lend slides in this way – you need to visit them to look at
the slides. But national indexes are increasingly going to work
in this way.

no provision for payment to the owner of the artwork copyright. Irrespective of the position under the copyright act, commission contracts should specify what the commissioner's rights are to use photographs or other images of the work.

Public art works which can not be defined as sculpture or works of artistic craftsmanship cannot be copied in this way. This would include a painted mural, but as with all definitions there are many grey areas – what of a mural made of painted ceramics or in bas-relief? Similarly sculpture or works of artistic craftsmanship which are in a public place but are not *permanently* sited there cannot be copied. A billboard, for example, whilst being in a public place is not a sculpture, a work of artistic craftsmanship nor is it permanently sited and thus falls outside this copyright exemption.

Slide indexes

The copying of artworks onto slides for indexes is subject to the same copyright legislation as any other form of copying. The copyright act makes provision for copying works and the supply of copies of works by libraries and archives to people who wish to use them for research or private study. The act does not distinguish between different types of copyright work in this context, so we must assume that what applies to literary works also applies to artworks. Library and archive copying is a permitted act under certain conditions, and it is regulated by specific provisions within copyright law.

see 8 • Permitted acts

Slide indexes can be sources of copyright infringement, particularly if slides are lent to users. When an artist places a slide on an index there should be a clear agreement about the conditions of use, including fees payable for reproduction by a third party, and whether the index takes any responsibility for copyright infringement arising from abuse of slides in their care. There should be a similar agreement between the index and any user.

Slides will usually be marked with the artists name, title of work and the date of completion or in some art forms the date of first publication but it is also worth including the © symbol before the artist's name.

Electronic storage of images

The act specifically provides that the storage of any literary, dramatic, artistic or musical work in any medium by electronic means, eg a database, constitutes an infringement of the copyright in that work; if it is a 'restricted act'. Because of this consent of the copyright owner must be given.

Once the image of the copyright work has been stored by electronic means, its retrieval on paper or other material form (eg slides) would also be a restricted act, and would constitute copyright infringement. If the retrieval is not in a permanent medium, for instance if it appears directly on a VDU screen, there is probably no copyright infringement, except where it is transmitted to subscribers, such as Ceefax and Prestel (regarded as inclusion in a cable programme for the purpose of the act). However this is of little practical importance given that the original loading of the image would constitute an infringement unless the copyright owner has consented.

Photo libraries

Photo libraries are similar to slide indexes though their intention is to sell work not to make it available for reference. A photographer will lodge work with a photo library who may actively promote it for editorial advertising or commercial use or may respond to inquiries from potential users. The user, say a newspaper, pays a fee to the library and the library pays the photographer. Photo agencies operate in a similar way except they commission photographs on their own behalf or behalf of clients.

By placing work with a library the photographer is obviously granting permission for it to be copied. The submission of work is in effect a licence. It can be exclusive, so only that library or agency can deal with the photograph (even the photographer can't sell it elsewhere) or non-exclusive so the photographer can deal directly with a client or place the same photograph with another library. Deciding whether to agree to an exclusive licence or not will depend on the fee offered and the library's ability to place work with clients. Any such agreement should specify that it is a licence for particular usage and that copyright has not been assigned but remains with the photographer. The right of authorship should be asserted and all prints clearly marked with title, photographers name, date of first publication and the © symbol.

Picture loan schemes

Any artist whose work is used by a picture or art loan scheme should have a clear agreement stating that copyright remains with the artist and asserting moral rights. As with selling or exhibiting, all work should be clearly marked with title, artists name, date of creation or first publication and the © symbol.

The picture loan scheme may want to copy work to keep a slide index or use for publicity and the agreement should be clear about what is and is not allowed for such purposes. The picture loan scheme should be equally clear in giving information to its members that borrowing work does not give them the right to copy.

5 • Licences & contracts

Copyright licences granted by the copyright owner permit someone else to copy an artwork – eg prints postcards, posters, use of photographic images of a work for commercial use. Assignment of copyright is different, it means actually transferring copyright ownership to someone else, whilst a licence simply permits limited acts of copying. Assignment or licensing of copyright may also apply to 'future copyright', ie it is possible for the artist to agree now to permit copying or to transfer copyright ownership of works not yet made. The copyright, and the

see 10 • Moral rights licence(s) comes into force on completion of the work. Moral rights are not transferable in the artist's lifetime, but will be transmitted on the death of the artist to the artist's heirs.

Licences

A licence is just one type of legal contract. It may be exclusive or non-exclusive.

An exclusive licence grants the sole reproduction rights to one person or organisation for specified purpose(s) and/or within specified territories. It would thus exclude all other persons *including the copyright owner* from copying the work for those purposes and within those territories. Because an artist who grants an exclusive license excludes him/herself from the reproduction rights granted, care must be taken to closely define the limitations of those rights. An exclusive licensee can sue for infringements of copyright. An exclusive licence must be made in writing.

A non-exclusive licence does not give sole reproduction rights to a single person or organisation but simply permits someone to reproduce a work for limited and defined purposes. Any number of non-exclusive licences in the same work can be issued by the copyright owner, even if they are for the same purposes and within the same territories. A non-exclusive licence can be verbal but it is strongly advisable to put it into writing to clearly specify the rights – for example what is being reproduced (ie title of the work), in what form (eg catalogue), for what purpose (eg retail sale), how many copies (eg edition of 5000), for how long (eg until edition is sold out), in what area (eg UK only), for what fee or royalty. Having all this in writing avoids difficulty of verification in the event of a dispute. A non-exclusive licensee cannot sue for infringements of copyright.

When considering limiting reproduction or sale rights to one or more countries, it is as well to know that EC law on the free movement of goods and services within EC member states makes it impossible to take legal action to prevent a licensee from exporting licensed copies to other countries, even if the licence prohibits this. EC law says that, once the copyright owner has authorised an article to be sold under his/her copyright (eg by licensing the copyright to someone else), then he/she can no longer use national copyright laws in other countries to prevent unauthorised imports into that country.

Example

A painter is approached by a firm that wishes to make a range of merchandise – cards, posters, wrapping paper, fabric – with the central image from one of the painter's works as the dominant motif. If the painter wishes the work to be copied for cards and posters only, not on wrapping paper and fabric, then the licence must reflect this. Another limitation might have to do with the places in which the copied work can be marketed. The painter might have political or moral reasons for wishing to exclude certain countries, so the licence can stipulate 'in the UK only'. Finally, the painter might feel a five year licence is reasonable, but beyond that time the work will become over-exposed, or out of date. The licence can reflect both place and time limitations. It is also possible to limit the number of copies permitted. In the case of casts from an original sculpture, or prints, there may be a physical limitation on the quality of repeated copies. Granting permission for one copy should not open the floodgates.

Apart from written or verbal licences there are also cases where, even if an artist has never expressly given permission for copying, this will be implied by circumstances. For example, an artist sends a press release to a magazine with a photograph. The artist has not expressly agreed, verbally or in writing, for the magazine to publish but permission will be implied by sending the press release and photograph.

Another example would be if an artist is told that a gallery intends making postcards of their work to sell when an exhibition ends, and does see 6 • Fees & royalties not complain or ask for royalties, the artist's permission may well be implied. In effect the gallery will have a non-exclusive licence to copy.

Verbal and implied contracts are open to misinterpretation. So always use a written contract to avoid later problems even if this is just a letter summing up a verbal agreement.

Checklist for a non-exclusive licence

For use when the copyright owner (normally the artist) permits a gallery, agent or publishing company to reproduce a piece of his/her work.

• Name/address/telephone number of gallery/agent/publisher.

• Name/address/telephone number of artist.

• Details of the work(s) to be reproduced (title, media, size, date).

• Form of reproduction (ie poster, postcard, calendar, book, greeting cards, etc).

• Method of reproduction (ie four colour process lithography, duotone, etc).

• Size of reproduction.

• Number of copies of the reproduction (ie, the print run).

• Other details of the product in or on which the work is to be reproduced.

• Whether the product is to be sold (if so how and at what price) or given as a gift (ie business Christmas cards).

• Statement that the agreement does not restrict the artist from licensing the same reproduction rights in the work to others (if it does restrict the artist it will be an exclusive licence).

• Is there an option for the publisher to increase the print run or to reprint and under what terms?

• Does the publisher have the right to keep the original work for the duration of the agreement? If so, does the artist have the right to borrow back the work for exhibition and have access to it to photograph it? If so, is the publisher obliged to insure the work for an agreed value?

• Does the agreement require the publisher to return the work, the transparencies, plate, negatives, etc after the agreed number of copies have been printed or the licence has ended?

Attribution

see 9 • Moral rights
• The artist should assert moral right of authorship and the licence should state the agreed form of accreditation that will appear on every copy.

• The licence should also state that every copy will bear the international copyright symbol © together with the Artist's name and date of first publication.

Integrity of Reproduction

• Will the work be reproduced in full without cropping, the superimposition of text, image, symbol or other mark, or does the agreement permit this (in which case full details should be given)?

• The agreement should give the artist the right to view proofs and refuse permission to publish if in his/her view the quality of reproduction is of an unacceptable standard.

Duration

• The licence must state how long the publisher has the right to reproduce the work without having to come back to the artist to renew or renegotiate the contract.

Payment

see 6 • Fees & royalties
• Is the artist paid royalties on sales (ie an agreed percentage of the wholesale or retail price)? If so what is the percentage? Does the artist have any say in the price at which the copies are sold?

• Or is the artist paid an agreed lump sum?

• Or is the fee to be a combination of royalties and lump sum?

• How and when payments are to be made?

• Does the artist have the right to a detailed royalty statement on a regular basis?

• Has the publisher guaranteed (in the case of royalties) that he will sell a minimum number per year?

• Signed (on behalf of the publisher)

• Signed (artist)

• Date

Partial assignment

see 'Assertion of moral rights', 9 • Moral rights

A little used and complicated method of exploiting your copyright is by a partial assignment which transfers part of copyright in a work to another person. The contract granting a partial assignment, which would need to be in writing, could set limitations on use and period of use but the 1988 copyright act rules out for assignments any limitations on territory – the rights have to be world-wide. Anyone entering into a partial assignment should seek legal advice.

Blanket licences

Blanket licences are copyright licences issued by a licensing body, using a licensing scheme. The best example of this is the educational use of material agreed by the Copyright Licensing Agency with universities and colleges. Licence fees are paid to the CLA which confers permission on users (ie students and staff) in the subscribing institutions to make copies for education purposes, but with certain limits. The CLA only covers the copying of books, learned journals, and periodicals on paper form. There are currently moves to bring artistic works within the CLA's brief.

see 'Design & Artists Copyright Society', 7 • Infringements of copyright

The Design and Artists Copyright Society operates a scheme that grants individual licences on behalf of visual artists.

The 1988 copyright act established the Copyright Tribunal (the old Performing Right Tribunal, with wider scope) to oversee schemes for licensing the reproduction of copyright works, and the actual forms of the licences themselves. Licensing schemes are subject to control by the Monopolies and Mergers Commission and provisions of the Fair Trading Act 1973. Much of the Copyright Tribunal's work will probably be concerned with adjudication on licensing matters.

Contracts generally

The problem of inadequate contractual agreement is endemic in the art world. A contract between artist and gallery, or a commission contract, is often unwritten, or is a short letter, or a simple agreement about percentage commission charged against sale price often not covering essential issues. Copyright is often not considered.

see 'Negotiating', 6 • Fees & royalties

All contracts should include the following provisions dealing with copyright and moral rights:
• Copyright belongs to the artist.
• That the artist asserts his/her moral right of authorship.

- The artist's name and the title of the work must always be displayed on or with the work or any copies of the work.
- What specific copying of the work, if any, is allowed (eg for an exhibition poster) and any fee involved – see licence checklist above.

A few other suggestions on how to conclude successful contracts are:

- Successful negotiation ensures the needs of both parties, not just one, are satisfied. It does not involve defeating the other party.
- Know as much as possible about the other party – eg what advances, royalties, fees have they given to others?
- Know as much as possible about what other artists have achieved in similar deals, and preferably get hold of a copy of their contract for comparison.
- See if you can borrow a sample contract or checklist from someone.
- Before negotiations write down the most important points you need to agree.
- Put all offers in writing.
- Be prepared, on occasions, to lose a deal rather than put up with one you will regret.
- Never leave it open to doubt whether you have agreed to a proposal or not – eg if a publisher writes to you setting out proposed terms and you do not reply, a contract may well be implied even if you didn't want to conclude one.
- Never agree to something, in writing or verbally, when you know you still have points to discuss and agree.
- When all the important issues are discussed and agreed, make sure these are embodied in a contract or exchange of letters, which is signed by both parties.
- Keep copies of all correspondence.
- Keep written notes of meetings and important phone conversations.
- Insist on signing a contract or exchanging letters before permitting any work (eg reproductions) to go ahead – it is much more difficult to negotiate from a position of weakness.
- Beware signing something which may later turn out to be a contract.

Many artists' opportunities come in the form of an open competition. Competition rules are a contractual agreement. A typical entry form may state that *'The selected artist shall assign to* (name of commissioning body) *full copyright in respect of the completed commission and all preparatory drawings.'* That applies to the successful winner of the competition. But the commissioner may claim the right to *'display and reproduce the submissions in the form of postcards, posters, books or other publicity materials without charge. Copyright, (in this case) shall, however, remain with the artist.'* The restrictions on the winning artist often also include the undertaking *'not to produce any replicas of the work without prior written approval.'*

In an entry form for a competition run in Scotland in 1990 there is no mention of moral rights, no provision for a limitation on the licensing of postcards, posters, etc, nor any agreement concerning reproduction right or royalty payments. The only concession to moral rights is the agreement that (the commissioner) *'will place near the commission a suitable plaque, with a wording to be agreed with the selected artist, describing the commission and naming the selected artist.'*

When filling in an entry form an artist can strike out such clauses or insert clauses detailing reproduction fee, etc. If the competition organisers accept your entry fee or work without objection to the deletion(s) then they may be taken to have agreed to the changes. The risk is that they will not and that your entry will not be accepted. Keep a photocopy of the form.

6 • Fees & royalties

by Simon Stern   The question artists most often ask about a proposed fee is *'Is it fair?'*. The fact is that fairness, in the ethical sense, seldom enters into decisions about fees. More useful questions to ask are: Is it acceptable to the artist in terms of time spent, publicity gained, or some other consideration? Is it the 'going rate'? Does it adequately reflect the value of the creator's work to the buyer?

Fees vary enormously according to the use to which the work is to be put and the market strength of the creator. For instance, an image for a greetings card may fetch £100 to £150; the same image used in advertising £1000 to £1500. The going rates for the two uses are different because the greetings card industry is over-supplied with willing artists and sells in a competitive environment; whereas advertising is supplied by a smaller number of specialists, usually represented by agents, and operates in an environment in which the cost of creating the image are as nothing compared to the costs of buying advertising space.

Types of fee

Flat fees

Flat fees are suitable where the licence being acquired is limited and defined – for instance an edition of calendars published by a company to send to its clients at Christmas. To the artist, the advantages of a flat fee are certainty about the amount he/she will get, and reasonably quick payment of the whole amount. Even if the proposed use is open ended, a flat fee may sometimes be suitable, eg if there are a lot of different contributors. In such cases the payment of royalties to all of them, each requiring the negotiation of a long and complicated contract, may be a practical impossibility.

Pete Fryer, *North Blyth Commission.* A photographic commission by Amber Films and Side Gallery, in response to a request from the North Blyth Campaign Committee to help fight Wansbeck Council 's proposal to re-develop the village of North Blyth for potential industry, and re-house the inhabitants elsewhere. The photographs were used as a local touring exhibition and as post cards for the campaign. They were also used by local and national newspapers and TV news broadcasts, as well as in Split Screen – a national 'community' TV programme. Pete Fryer was paid by Split Screen and the national newspapers, but not by TV news or local papers. Local newspapers would not have credited him as photographer if he had not insisted. TV news is not required to credit under the provisions of 'fair dealing'.

Repeat fees

In some cases there may be a flat fee for an initial use such as, fabric, with the possibility of further uses if the design is a success – wallpaper, lampshades and so forth. Or, to continue with the fabric example, the initial fee may be for one season, with the possibility that the design will be sold in subsequent seasons. In such cases a repeat flat fee may be negotiated. A repeat fee can be defined in several ways: as a percentage of the original fee (this is a wasting asset for the artist because of inflation and so is not suitable for long-term agreements); 'to be agreed' when the occasion arises (which gives flexibility, but also uncertainty); or, if the original producer is selling on rights to a third party, as a percentage of the sum received (for instance in the case of a book cover for the UK edition, where a USA publisher buys the right to use it on the USA edition from the UK publisher). This last is half way to a royalty, which is the third, and most complicated form of payment.

Royalties

Royalties are a form of payment which gives the creator a continuing stake in the success of the product. Payments are usually expressed as a percentage of the retail (published) price or wholesale price (actual amounts received) of the product, which deals with the inflation problem. Royalties expressed as 'x pence per copy' are only suitable for short term agreements where inflation is not a significant factor.

If the original producer/publisher has the right to sell on rights to other producers/publishers (for instance, the UK publisher selling the USA rights) then the creator will also get a substantial proportion of these 'rights' sales.

It is customary to pay a proportion of the royalties in advance as a lump sum. The advance should be in the region of half the royalty value of the first printing/manufacture. The higher the advance, the greater the confidence the publisher/producer is expressing in the product. Advances are customarily not returnable, even if sales of the product never cover them. The artist should bear in mind that the advance may be the only payment he/she will see if the venture is not a success. Thus the artist on royalties generally takes on some of the risk (since the advance on a royalty is usually less than a flat fee would be) as well as standing to gain from successes.

It follows from all this that royalties are not a particularly suitable form of payment where there is no potential to sell a lot of copies – eg, in the case of a (genuine) limited edition, or a seasonal design with a finite life.

Artists entering royalty agreements should always seek expert advice, or read up on the subject. They often involve very long-term relationships, and are complicated documents. Here are the main snags to look out for:

see 'Checklist for a
non-exclusive
licence', 5 • Licences
& contracts

• Payment should be based on retail price, or 'actual amounts received', never on amounts received less cost of manufacture, as this is too vague.

• The publisher/producer should undertake to publish/produce within a defined period.

• The rights should revert to the creator if the product goes out of print/out of production.

• The creator's accountant should have the right to inspect the accounts of the publisher/producer.

• There should be set times for payment.

• The creator's copyright should be declared on the image/product.

• The artist should have confidence in the probity of the publisher/manufacturer.

The amount of royalty is usually between 5% and 20%; 10% is the standard payment for books. But royalty payments are always negotiable. In the case of sales of rights (as described above) the creator should get at least 50%, often more.

Negotiating

see 'Contracts generally', 5 • Licences & contracts

Artists are often not experienced negotiators, so here are a few guidelines:

- All contracts are negotiable. Royalty contracts especially so.
- The commissioner's first offer is almost never his/her best.
- Never let yourself be put on the spot. Prepare a few get-out phrases such as *'I'll have to get back to you about that'.*
- Consult your friends, especially the more successful ones.
- Get your aims and fall-back position clear in your mind.
- To negotiate successfully, you must be prepared to lose the job. (You would be amazed what good deals you can get when you genuinely don't want it).
- Don't be afraid of silence. Listen, and get a good understanding of the other side's aims and resources.
- Remain calm, but firm at all times. Take your time.
- Make a note of all matters agreed, date it, and keep it.

7 • Infringements of copyright

The copyright owner has the legal right to prevent unauthorised persons from committing an infringement.

There are two kinds of infringement:

• Primary infringement – someone commits a 'restricted act' – ie copies an artistic work in any form, issues copies to the public, or broadcasts or includes the work in a cable service, or authorises someone else to do any of these things.

• Secondary infringement – someone does not actually copy or authorise the copying, but knowingly imports illegal copies or possesses or deals in illegal copies as part of a business, this includes providing premises or apparatus for making illegal copies.

see also 8 • Permitted acts Primary infringers are generally liable even when they are not aware they are infringing copyright. Secondary infringers are liable if they have any reason to believe they are dealing in infringing copies.

To succeed in legal action the copyright owner must show that the copying is 'substantial'. If an essential element of the work is copied that will be substantial even if it is a physically small part. The test is whether the copier has used a substantial part of the 'skill and labour' of the original maker.

It is not necessary to show that the copier has intended to copy. Innocent copying can still be an infringement. Nor is there any need to prove that the copyright owner has suffered 'damage', although this will affect how much money a court will award.

Copying specifically includes the making of a three-dimensional copy of a two-dimensional work and vice versa – eg a drawing of a sculpture.

The 'restricted acts' of primary infringement do not include exhibiting the work without the copyright owner's permission. No artist can prevent one of their works being shown in public unless this is prohibited under a contract with the exhibitor. Also there must be actual

Objects of Desire by Sitespecific, **commissioned by Artangel Trust as one of a series of works using Spectacolour boards** *Objects of Desire* **was 'used' by a pop group Spacemen 3 and reconstituted as a promo video. The artists are pursuing legal action for compensation. Artangel's policy in all projects is that it retains the right to use documentation for publicity purposes but copyright of all material remains with the artist. Sitespecific are** Andy Parkin, Bruce Williams **and** Chris McHugh.
Photo: *John Carson*

reproduction by the infringer and this would not be so if an artist incorporated in their own work an existing copy or reproduction of another artist's work – eg in a collage.

In both cases of primary and secondary infringement the copyright owner, or exclusive licensee, can take civil proceedings (usually in a county court) against the infringer.

Offering for sale or hire or certain other commercial dealing in articles that infringe copyright is a criminal act under section 107 of the 1988 copyright act if the seller or hirer knew or had reason to believe the articles were infringing copies. Commercial dealing includes exhibiting works in public in the course of business. The penalties (imprisonment and fining) offer the artist greater protection than under the previous 1956 act. But they are rarely used – one of the problems is persuading the police to be interested! Private criminal prosecutions, though possible, are extremely rare. If an infringement dispute reaches the stage of going to court a civil action is still the realistic remedy.

An artist whose copyright has been infringed could first approach the infringer to see if an amicable settlement can be arranged. A further step would be to use a solicitor's letter. If such 'softly softly' approaches do not work a copyright owner can take civil proceedings in a court (normally a county court) for:

- In appropriate cases an injunction, for example to prevent someone who has illegally copied work from dealing in it or to stop someone already dealing in work from selling more copies.

- Damages to compensate the artist for the loss suffered (often based on lost profits or royalties).

- Sometimes an account of the profits the copier has made by copying or 'exemplary damages' where the infringement has been flagrant.

- The delivery up and destruction of infringing articles.

With moral rights, an action may be brought against the person responsible, for breach of 'statutory duty'. The remedies open to an artist are roughly as for copyright infringement but an injunction will only be available for breaches of the 'right of integrity' (ie to prevent derogatory treatment of a work) and even here only when a disclaimer is not made disassociating the artist from the treatment of the work.

Getting legal advice

Professional legal advice from a solicitor should always be taken in situations likely to involve a court action. A solicitor's advice can also be very useful to prevent a case having to come to court. A solicitor's letter is a useful tool in dealing with a copyright infringer. Remember legal proceedings in a court can be very expensive. Legal aid may be available as well as the Green Form scheme, which can give up to two hours free advice from a solicitor. Ask a solicitor or the Citizens Advice Bureau for advice.

Free legal advice is available from Citizens Advice Bureaux and other advice centres. This can be extremely useful but remember copyright is a specialist area and the advice centre solicitor may not have copyright experience. They also will not be able to act for you if you take it further. They may be able to refer you local solicitors specialising in copyright. Law centres may be able to offer help or refer you to a local solicitor. Contact the Law Centres Federation for a list of centres in your area.

The best way to find a solicitor is by personal recommendation. see 16 • Contacts Reference libraries have *The Solicitors Regional Directories* which list all solicitors in the area. This describes the type of work they do but doesn't include a category for copyright. You can also refer to Yellow Pages under 'solicitors'.

Questions to ask a solicitor

Although not many solicitors are experts in copyright or familiar with artists' problems, you will not always require specialist advice. Here are a few questions to help find a solicitor who is competent, interested in your case and affordable:

- Ask for a short initial meeting or phone conversation free of charge to explain the problem and find out how the solicitor thinks they can help. You should not expect any free advice at this meeting.
- Before seeing the solicitor assemble any correspondence and notes in date order and leave a copy with the solicitor.
- Establish at the first meeting if you are eligible for legal aid or the Green Form scheme. This will depend on your financial situation.
- Ask for an overall estimate of fees and an hourly rate.
- Make your own financial position clear.
- Ask who in the solicitor's office you will deal with – you may find it is someone straight out of law school and this may be fine in some cases.
- In a case where specialist advice is needed ask what kind of work the solicitor usually does and the kind of clients they act for.
- Do not hesitate to make a decision based on personal impressions. Having a solicitor you like and can work with is important.
- Discuss the alternatives with your solicitor – expediency, time and cost can sometimes be more important than principle.
- Keep in regular contact with the solicitor to keep up to date with progress. Do not encourage your solicitor to write you long letters of advice as these cost money and often leave you none the wiser. Telephone calls or short meetings are often better.
- Respond promptly to telephone calls and letters and tell your solicitor if you are unclear about advice or your case generally.

Avoiding legal action

Prevention is a lot better than cure and the best ways of avoiding legal action are:

- Always use a written contract.
- In cases where copyright is being transferred or any copies or reproductions permitted always ensure a proper licence or assignment has been signed, which covers all relevant matters.
- Always assert your moral rights.
- Always keep a careful watch for copyright or moral rights infringements and act promptly in all cases.
- Consider joining the appropriate rights society, according to whether it is an artistic work, work of literature or drama, or a performance.

Design and Artists Copyright Society

DACS is the British copyright collecting society for the visual arts. It is a non-profit making society formed by artists in 1984 to administer and protect the copyright in all visual artist's work. DACS is able to represent in the UK some 20,000 artists in matters of copyright by reciprocal and unilateral agreements with similar societies worldwide. Members of DACS get the same consideration and protection abroad, to the extent of each national law. DACS protects artists' copyright by actively pursuing unauthorised reproductions of their members' work and, when appropriate, taking up their cases in law. DACS administers copyright by licensing anyone who wishes to reproduce a work of visual art in any medium. Fees charged for the reproduction of a copyright work are from a standard published tariff.

8 • Permitted acts

The copyright act allows for a number of precisely defined exemptions to the general rule preventing copying of a copyright work. 'Fair dealing' forms one set of these exemptions the purpose of which is to honour the principle that copyright should not hinder the acquisition of knowledge. Other exemptions apply to some very specific circumstances under which copyright works are made or exhibited.

Fair dealing

The act defines three forms of fair dealing:

- for research or private study;
- for criticism or review; and
- for the reporting of current events.

It is permissible for copies to be made of copyright works, without permission, in these circumstances but the copying must be 'fair', ie not exploitative. In assessing fairness both the amount of the work copied, the motive of the copier and whether its use competes with the copyright owner will be taken into account.

Research & private study uses

'Research' means research by any individual for any purpose, including commercial research. 'Private study' means study other than as part of the work of an educational establishment. Research applies to all artistic, and other works, except sound recordings, films, videos and broadcast or cable TV programmes, which are covered by special provisions, ie licences negotiated through the Copyright Licensing Authority. Only single copies may be made and no acknowledgement of authorship is required.

Criticism & review

The exemption for 'criticism & review' applies to all copyright works. It means any legitimate critical study or review of a work, whether in the press or in an academic context, however, copies may not be made of substantial parts of a work. The Publishers Association and Society of Authors have worked out an agreement that allows for up to 8,000 words from a novel or 10% of the whole. In music, eight bars seems to be accepted as a reasonable extract from a symphony. These proportions

Yolanda Christian, *Tree of Life*, oil on canvas, 18"x22". *'This image was used for a review in the Birmingham Post, where it suffered being clumsily cropped rather than being simply reduced. If the composition is spoilt, presumably the artist and reader are disserviced. At the time 'Taking Root' was being exhibited at the Midlands Art Centre where I was also interviewed by an art critic and televised for First Night, Central TV. Ironically I realised everyone had received payment except for me, the source material for this event! If I had not been so exhausted after hanging 50 works, I certainly would have challenged the lack of payment, but should I have to? On a previous occasion, the BBC World Service automatically paid me for a radio interview, which was broadcast across China... that's the way it should be.'*

are not substantial parts. The calculation of what is a substantial part is a matter of these generally accepted 'rules of thumb', and is not quantified in the act. No guidelines exist in the case of artistic works. A critic could hardly show 10% of a painting.

The exemption for criticism and review permits multiple copies in for example newspapers, magazines or books but it requires an acknowledgement identifying the work and its author.

The provisions of fair dealing		
Purpose	Art forms	Conditions
Research or private study	literary, dramatic, musical or artistic work	Single copies only permitted No acknowledgement of author necessary
Criticism or review	All works	Multiple copies permitted, eg newspapers, magazines and books Acknowledgement necessary
Reporting current events	All art forms except photography	Multiple copies permitted Acknowledgement required except when used in a sound recording, film, broadcast or cable programme

Reporting of current events

Fair dealing applies to journalistic reporting of current events, that is anything deemed to be newsworthy and/or in the public interest. This is a fairly contentious area, and newspapers would probably fight for the right to determine what is and what is not a 'current event'. Artistic works and live events may be included in film or photography or sound recordings that are made for the purpose of reporting current events. An exception is made for photographs, which may not be copied under this provision, to prevent the abuse of photographers' rights.

Multiple copies are permitted and acknowledgement of authorship is required, but not when the copy is used in sound recording, film, TV broadcasting, cable etc. Apparently those responsible for current affairs in the broadcast media persuaded the government that crediting copyright owners in a 'news' or current affairs programme would be too much trouble.

Educational use

Copying in educational establishments is closely differentiated, according to the purpose for which it is required. There are also licensing agreements covering copying for educational purposes.

What may or may not be copied for educational purposes is complex. Blanket licensing schemes operated by the CLA cover some copying for use in schools and colleges. The 1988 act also permits some copying for educational purposes, but the rules vary according to the category of work, with special provisions for broadcast and cable TV.

The act makes it clear that copying of artworks by students as part of their education is permitted even if the original is still under copyright, on the following conditions:

- The copying must not involve any reprographic process (photocopying or other mechanical copying technique)
- The copying is done by the person giving or receiving the instruction.

The tradition of art students copying artworks by hand is not an infringement, it only becomes so if such copies are subsequently *'dealt with'*, ie *'sold or let for hire, or offered or exposed for sale or hire'*.

Performances done for 'instruction' in an educational establishment do not infringe copyright.

Incidental inclusion in another work

This provides that there will be no copyright infringement by incidental inclusion of one copyright work in another work. 'Incidental' probably means not central to the main work. This exemption applies to all works, but it permits the copied work to be included only in an artistic work, sound recording, film, broadcast or cable programme. Copies may be issued to the public, or the work broadcast or shown in public or in a cable programme service. This exemption would permit, for example, a painting which appeared on the wall of a film set to be included in a broadcast drama without the consent of the owner of the copyright in the painting. Specifically excluded from this category of fair dealing is any form of music or words and music which has been 'deliberately included'. Presumably this refers to the ability in filming a documentary to control the sound recording, even if the inclusion of visual artworks cannot be avoided.

This category seems to have been designed specifically to assist documentary photography or film-making. It has been pointed out by some authorities that it could not apply to incidental inclusion of an artistic work in an advertising film, because as the director would have complete control over the camera, nothing would be incidental.

Anonymous or pseudonymous works

There is no infringement if it is not possible, by reasonable inquiry, to identify the artist and if it is reasonable to assume the copyright has expired or that the artist died more than fifty years ago.

Other permitted acts

Three additional permitted acts apply specifically to artistic works:

• Sculpture and works of artistic craftsmanship permanently situated in public or in premises to which the public has access may be photographed, filmed, drawn or painted without permission from the copyright owner and copies issued to the public. Works which are not sculptures or works of artistic craftsmanship or that are not permanently sited in public cannot be copied, eg paintings, painted murals and billboards. Premises open to the public include museums and galleries. This is one reason why a common condition of entry to galleries and museums is that photographs cannot be taken. Any photographing will not then be a copyright infringement but a breach of contract between gallery and members of the public enabling the gallery to take to court anyone who ignores the condition and, for example, sells prints of the photograph to the public.

see 'Catalogues' & 'Postcards & posters', 4 • The uses of copyright

• Copies may be made of an artistic work for the purposes of advertising the sale of the work. Reproductions made for this purpose may be made prior to the sale of the work. Once the work has been offered for sale, and whether it is sold or not, further use – ie subsequent sale of the catalogue or brochure – would be an infringement. This provision is new. It is quite restrictive. First, it only applies to copies made to advertise the sale of the work itself, and not to copies made to advertise the sale of copies, reproductions or a book or catalogue which includes a copy of a drawing. Secondly, once the work is sold the exemption will not apply, so for instance catalogues or posters produced for an exhibition of works for sale cannot be sold without the permission of the copyright owner once the exhibition is over. Thirdly, even if it is permissible to copy a work for this purpose, if a permitted copy is later sold, exhibited in public or distributed, it will be treated as an infringing copy and the person responsible can still be guilty of secondary infringement.

- An artist may make a copy of a previous work, when copyright has been assigned to another person, provided that the main design of the previous work is not imitated. The precise meaning of this section of the act is obscure but it should allow the production of a series with the same theme if the main design is not repeated.

9 • Moral rights

Angela Edmonds, *The Grand Staircase*.
Angela Edmonds had an exhibition at Moor Park Golf Club. She included titles and prices under each work. The labelling was removed by the club and replaced with a sign saying, *'Please enquire at the reception desk if you are interested in purchasing any of my work'*. The exhibition coincided with the Wang Tennis Tournament and was a good selling opportunity. But she felt *'My work was used to embellish the Arnhem Room for the Wang Tournament while denying me the opportunity to sell by removing titles and prices. To add insult to injury the works were clearly visible in a promotional video... which appeared on television'*. It was before 1 August 1989 so she had no recourse to the moral rights provision of the 1988 act which would have given the right to have her name on each work but not the right to have the price displayed.

The importance of copyright in practice lies in the values, both tangible and intangible, attached to the original work. Ownership of copyright gives an author ownership of an 'intellectual property'. This form of property ownership should allow control of any economic exploitation of the work – through copying – in the market place. The danger is that, in dealing with artistic works purely

73

Geraldine Walsh, **untitled drawing, charcoal and chalk on board.** Images can quite legitimately be cropped to show a detail provided the need for this is obvious and it is credited as a detail. In the bottom image though, the drawing has been turned through 90° and there is no caption describing it as a detail. This could be taken as an example of derogatory treatment as it misrepresents the drawing. Another artist, **Helen Ganly, had some of her drawings returned from a publisher cut up – the publisher had 'cropped' the drawings by actually trimming them to fit them on the page. They then became unexhibitable. This is** another example of derogatory treatment. **Helen Ganly feels that when she illustrates books for younger children, where she is also the writer, her professional status as an artist is taken seriously – when she illustrates for older readers she feels it is not.**

as commodities, an important second concept will be overlooked – an author's 'moral rights'. These relate to a work's intrinsic, rather than extrinsic or market value. They may protect an artist's reputation, the work's meaning and artistic integrity.

Moral rights currently exist in over 70 countries. Until the passing of the 1988 act, they did not materially exist in the United Kingdom. Introduction of moral rights was a condition of the UK ratifying the Berne Convention.

As with copyright, moral rights persist even when the actual work has passed into someone else' possession.

In the 1988 copyright act four moral rights are granted:

- The right to be identified as author (or director in the case of a film or video) of a work. This right must be asserted in writing, or it is lost.
- The right to object to derogatory treatment of a work.
- The right to prevent false attribution of a work to the artist.
- The right (of a person commissioning a photograph, film or video) to maintain the privacy of the work that has been made for purely private reasons, eg family events.

see 'Commissions and employment', 2 • Who owns copyright

Moral rights in a work produced by an employee in the course of employment belongs to the employer, not to the employee/artist. Although these are the statutory rights there is nothing to stop artists and others including moral rights clauses in their contracts (eg public commissions) which go beyond the statutory rights. At the very least in all contracts the moral right of authorship should be asserted.

Right of authorship

Also known as the right of paternity, this gives the artist the right to be identified whenever an artistic work is published commercially, exhibited in public, a visual image of it is broadcast or included in a film or (in the case of sculptures or works of artistic craftsmanship only) whenever copies of a graphic work (eg a painting or drawing), or a photograph of it are issued to the public. The artist has the right to be identified in a clear and prominent manner, using any reasonable form of identification. But where the artist in asserting the right specifies initials or pseudonym, or other means of identification this must be used instead.

If you want the authorship of your works acknowledged you must assert this (the other moral rights do not have to be asserted). In the case of an artwork exhibited in public if an artist has his/her name or signature visible on the work or copy or on the work's frame or mount when the artist parts with possession of the original, there is an obligation upon anyone into whose hands the work passes in effect to reinstate the author's identification if it has been obscured or lost. This also applies to copies made by the artist or under the artist's control. In any case other than the public exhibition of works the assertion must be in writing, either in any assignment of copyright or in any other 'instrument in writing' signed by the artist, eg a contract or licence.

An acceptable form of words that asserts the moral right of authorship is:

'The right of (name of author/artist) to be identified as author of (identify work) has been asserted generally in accordance with sections 77 and 78 of the Copyright, Designs and Patents Act 1988.'

Section 77 describes the right, and section 78 states the requirement for it to be asserted.

It is not always enough to ensure that the right has been asserted in this way as only certain people will be affected or bound by it:

- In the case of works publicly exhibited, anyone into whose hands the work, or copy, passes is automatically bound.

- When copyright is assigned, the assignee, and anyone who acquires or licenses copyright from the assignee, is bound.

- Where the assertion is a statement in another written document signed by the artist (eg a licence, gallery or commission contract) only people made aware of the assertion are bound by it; this is why it is common to see a statement asserting an author's rights on the fly-leaf of most books published since 1 August 1989.

- Where the assertion is included in a copyright licence anyone possessing a licensed copy is automatically bound in relation to the public exhibition of the work, even if unaware of the assertion in the original licence.

Artists should always assert their rights promptly, otherwise they may lose any remedy they would have had. Anyone not giving the necessary credit should be written to promptly by the artist asserting the right of authorship.

The right of authorship does not apply to use of works in reporting current events or for publication in newspaper or magazines, or to works incidentally included in another work, or to the exploitation of designs derived from artistic works. There are other exceptions in the act.

The right of authorship lasts for the artist's life plus 50 years.

Right of integrity

This is the right to object to any 'derogatory treatment' of the work. This may be brought about by anything added to, taken away from, or any alteration to, or adaptation of the work, but in every case the change must amount to a distortion or mutilation of the work, or something which otherwise prejudices the artist's honour and reputation.

The right of integrity has not, at the date of publication, been tested in court but is likely to be looked at very narrowly by the courts, who will look objectively for evidence of reputation being affected.

Significantly, the right of integrity does not prevent the destruction of a work, nor the re-location of a work, for example a piece of site-specific public sculpture. This apparent lack of protection against a fundamental form of 'treatment' of an artistic work is surprising. In the well documented case of the Graham Sutherland portrait of Sir Winston Churchill, destroyed on the orders of Lady Churchill because she disliked it, even if this had happened after the 1988 act came into force nothing could have been done by the artist. Also there is no obligation to ensure that the owner of an artwork maintains it, even if lack of maintenance (eg hanging a tapestry in brilliant sunlight) would lead to its disrepair and have a possible harmful effect on the artist's reputation. It also appears that an artist may have no right to object to what appears to be derogatory treatment of a work in the course of 'legitimate restoration'. This interpretation must be disappointing to everyone concerned with works of art. The right of integrity does not apply to use

Carole Anne Rice – Writer by Ming de Nasty at **Poseurs Ming de Nasty and Rhonda Wilson specialise in portrait photographs at Poseurs in Birmingham. Before 1 August 1989 the commissioner of any photograph or portrait owned copyright. Under the 1988 copyright act the photographer owns copyright. Poseurs never use a photograph if the sitter asks them not to. This is a sensitive issue where correct legal practice may not be 'good' practice. It is important to be clear if the sitter objects to certain uses of the portrait. Then any agreement is founded in mutual respect.**

of works in reporting current events or for publication in newspapers or magazines. There are other exceptions similar to those applying to the right of authorship.

The right of integrity lasts for the artist's life plus 50 years.

Right to prevent false attribution

This permits an author to disclaim work wrongly attributed to them. The right is infringed by the public exhibition of the work, or a copy of the work, which is falsely attributed. There is a special provision in the 1988 act which applies only to artistic works: the right is infringed by someone who, in the course of a business, deals with a work which has been altered after the artist parted with possession of it in such a way as appears that it is the unaltered work of the original artist. This also applies to copies of the work.

For example after the death of her husband, an artist's widow saw one of his works offered for sale by his old gallery. She was made curious by the title, which she knew to have been the title of a work her husband had left unfinished at his death. She realised it was indeed the unfinished work, but someone else had completed it. She objected to the alteration, by the addition of another person's marks, which she felt demeaned the work. She also objected to the impression given by the work's existence that her husband might have more works as yet undiscovered, which suggested that she, as his heir, was releasing onto the market works which she had held back. She was unable to get the gallery either to withdraw the painting or to alter its attribution to her late husband. As heir to her husband's estate, under the new act, she would have also inherited his moral rights to refute authorship and it seems likely that she would have been able to prevent the false attribution because of the special provision in the new act referred to above.

The right of refuting authorship unlike other moral rights lasts for the artist's life plus 20 years.

Right of privacy

This applies in the case of privately commissioned photographs, film or video works. It only applies to the whole or a substantial part of a work.

It is mainly relevant to the misuse of private photographs (eg of a wedding) by the media. The right of privacy lasts for the artist's life plus 50 years.

Waiver of moral rights

Moral rights are personal and may not be assigned to another person. On the death of an artist they will pass to the artist's estate. They cannot be sold or licensed for another person to own. The moral rights of the author over a work continue to exist even when the copyright has been sold or licensed. However, the act specifically says that moral rights may be waived, either conditionally or unconditionally, or be subject to revocation.

A matter of concern is that, because moral rights can be 'waived', some contracts for artists' work will include a standard clause demanding this.

Any attempt by a gallery or commissioner to put pressure on artists to sign away their moral rights in contracts should be resisted. In the theatre, trade unions are resisting similar attempts to limit authors' moral rights to the single right to have their name removed from publicity if they object to the treatment of the work.

Even whilst the 1988 act was passing through Parliament, managements were attempting to get writers to sign 'Moral Rights' clauses that were, in effect, waivers of those rights. The Writers' Guild instructed its members to strike such clauses out of their contracts. Striking a clause out of a contract is a simple matter, but it must be done before both parties have signed the contract. The other signatory to the contract, the commissioner, purchaser or whoever, may not accept this action, which means that negotiations must begin.

Quite apart from specific written waivers, under the general law of contract, moral rights can be waived verbally or a waiver may be implied from the surrounding circumstances.

One problem for artists is the use of open competition as a major form of commissioning. Typically, an entry form for an open competition will be the only form of written agreement between artist and 'commissioner'. An artist's signature on a competition entry form regulations would be taken as a waiver of moral rights if a waiver clause was included or could be implied. A written assertion of moral rights could be attached to a competition entry form and any waiver clause struck out. However the risk would be that the entry could be refused.

Moral rights over parts of a work

The right of integrity and the right to prevent false attribution apply to any part of the work, however small; whereas the right of authorship (paternity) applies to the whole or a 'substantial' part of a work.

10 • Designs, patents & trade marks

The 1988 copyright act made important changes to the law on industrial designs. Under the previous law the principal means of protecting industrial designs from illegal exploitation was through the copyright protection given to the original design drawings on which the industrial articles were based. In addition some novel or original designs were registrable under the Registered Designs Act 1949 and protected for up to fifteen years. The 1988 copyright act has largely removed the copyright protection but has introduced a new unregistered right – design right. The registration of certain designs – registered designs – under the 1949 act continues but with the period of protection increased.

The interaction of the three rights – copyright, design right and registered design right – is complicated and specialist advice may be needed.

Copyright

Copyright protection for original artistic works normally lasts for the artist's life plus 50 years but if the artistic work has been industrially exploited, either by the artist or with his/her consent, then copyright protection is cut down to 25 years from when the articles are first marketed. Industrial exploitation means copying the artistic work by an industrial process and marketing the resulting articles in the UK or elsewhere. So an artist who paints a picture of a chair and later licenses someone else to exploit the design industrially, by making multiple three-dimensional copies of the chair from the painting, will then have their copyright protection cut down to 25 years from that date. Drawings which are used as the basis for designs which are made into articles no longer attract copyright protection at all – they are treated as 'design documents'.

Design right

This new right, like copyright, comes into existence automatically, no registration is needed. It protects certain eligible three-dimensional designs against commercial copying and relates to any aspect of the shape or configuration of an article.

Design right is automatically first owned by the designer (artist) unless it has been commissioned – then the commissioner is the original owner of the design right. This has obvious implications for public art commissions. If the designer is employed to do the work under a contract of service, the employer is first owner of the design right.

As with copyright, design right may be assigned or licensed to others.

The act defines 'design' as *'any aspect of the shape or configuration (whether internal or external) of the whole or part of an article'*. Design right doesn't exist in:

• A method or principle of construction.

• Features of shape or configuration enabling an article to be connected to another article to perform its function (known as 'must-fit' cases).

• Features of shape or configuration which are dependent on another article of which the design forms an integral part (known as 'must-match' cases).

• Surface decoration.

The term of protection in most cases will be ten years from first marketing of the design. If marketing is delayed for more than five years there is an alternative term of fifteen years from the date of first marketing the design.

The right is only exclusive during the first five years. During the final five years anyone will be entitled to a 'licence of right' to make and sell articles copying the design on royalty and other terms settled, if necessary, by the Comptroller of Patents, Designs and Trade Marks.

To qualify for design right a design must be 'original'. It must not be commonplace in the design field in question at the time. This originality requirement will be harder to show than for copyright.

There are complicated provisions as to who qualifies for design right protection and, because design right does not benefit from the Berne Convention, international protection will be restricted. Broadly speaking, designs made by individuals and companies outside the EC are excluded unless that country confers reciprocal protection for UK designs.

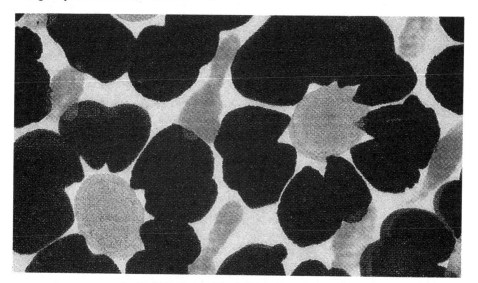

Janice Tchalenko, *Black Rose*. This design is from a series of pots and tableware Janice Tchalenko designed for Dart Pottery at Totnes in Devon.

Any three-dimensional design, such as a new teapot design, that is commercially exploited is automatically covered by design right – providing its shape isn't dictated solely by its function. Design right will protect the article for fifteen years from making the design drawing or a prototype, or ten years from first marketing the design, whichever is the shorter. Five years after first marketing anyone has the right to reproduce under licence but they have to pay the owner of the design right a fee. A two dimensional design cannot be protected in this way. It is covered by copyright and, if commercially exploited, protected for twenty-five years after first marketing.

Both a two and a three-dimensional design can be registered though. The design must not have been published or offered for sale before applying for registration – though you could display it at a trade show. Protection lasts for a maximum of fifteen years. Its value is three-fold:
• it applies to both two and three dimensional designs
• it gives you a monopoly of manufacture
• it protects you against 'independent' creation of the same design and not just manufacture.
With both registered and unregistered design right the commissioner owns the design right.

Design right is infringed, like copyright, by any copying of the design so as to produce articles the same, or substantially the same, as the original.

Registered designs

Certain designs intended for industrial application may be registered at the Patent Office under the 1949 Registered Designs Act, provided they possess some 'eye appeal'. 'Design' covers *features of shape, configuration, pattern or ornament applied to an article by any industrial process, being features which in the finished article appeal to and are judged by the eye'*. It doesn't include:

• A method of principle or construction.
• Features of shape or configuration which are dictated solely by the function of the article (ie functional articles).
• Features of shape or configuration which are dependent on the appearance of another article which the design is part of (known as 'must-match' cases).

You cannot register a design if:

• Aesthetic considerations are not normally taken into account to a 'material extent' by users of the article made from the design.
• Another application has been made for the same design.
• The design has been published in the UK before the application.
• The design differs from another design in 'immaterial' details or features which are *'variants commonly used in the trade'*.

The benefit of registering a design, as opposed to relying simply on design right or copyright, is that registration brings the designer exclusive rights of manufacture, sale and hire of articles made from the design. So there is no need to prove copying, and a person may infringe even when they don't know of the registered design.

Applications for the registration of designs should be made to the Patent Office. There is a fee, payable under the Registered Designs (Fees) Rules 1990, ranging from £30 to £50. The booklet *Applying to Register a Design* is available from the Patents Office and gives all necessary information. In order to be registered the design must be 'applied industrially' – ie be reproduced, or intended to be, in more than fifty articles.

see 16 • Contacts

According to the Patent Office's official definition the following are excluded from design registration:

- works of sculpture – other than casts or moulds used, or intended to be used, as models or patterns to be multiplied by any industrial process;
- wall plaques, medals and medallions; and
- printed matter primarily of a literary or artistic character including: book-jackets, calendars, certificates, coupons, dressmaking patterns, greetings cards, labels, leaflets, maps, plans, playing cards, postcards, stamps, trade advertisements, trade forms and cards, transfers, etc.

These types of works will be accorded copyright protection, but not design right. There is also a specific exclusion of an article designed as a functional part of another object. This would presumably exclude a door handle or knocker, or types of kitchen fittings.

It is in this area of 'artistic craftsmanship' that most of the problems of differentiating between copyright and design right will occur. Artists and crafts makers who intend to market their designs in quantity will want to take advantage of registered design right protection. But as the list above and the various limitations of design right application show, it may not necessarily be possible to gain registration.

Registered design affords protection up to a maximum of twenty five years for designs registered after 1 August 1989. It is possible to register corresponding designs overseas under an international convention.

Use of old designs

Designs held in company archives over longer periods of time usually have a non-registered, non-copyright status. They are in the public domain if they were first marketed more than 25 years ago.

Some firms have their own design archives, like Sandersons the wallpaper makers who acquired important Victorian wood-block designs by buying up the William Morris Factory, which are now technically in the public domain and so available to anyone to copy.

Stoddards, the carpet manufacturers, hold an original design commissioned from Charles Rennie Mackintosh. Copyright on Mackintosh's work would have been held in any case by the commissioner, and will have expired many years ago – he died in 1928. Naturally companies with valuable design archives will guard them from competitors. The Victoria and Albert Museum holds the world's most comprehensive textile design archive, which is available to designers.

The registration of a new design based on older ones depends on a decision by the Registrar of Designs, who will judge its originality. The managing director of a leading firm of silk printers has said *'We sometimes build a single design from sections culled from several different originals, enlarging or reducing them as the designer thinks fit.'*

Design right, registered design or copyright

The general principles are relatively simple but the effect on actual practice is complex and varied.

Copyright protection is now limited but sculpture and works of artistic craftsmanship still qualify for twenty five years protection if they are exploited industrially.

An artwork that is defined as sculpture is specifically excluded from registered design right, and is unlikely to qualify anyway by virtue of the small quantity produced (less than fifty examples). Design right, like copyright, is automatic. It doesn't give such good protection as copyright as it normally only lasts for ten years and does not cover surface decoration. But it will cover articles that copyright doesn't cover because they are not considered artistic works – eg a teapot to be manufactured in large quantities (more than 50 examples)

Registered design right covers a wider range of design (it includes two-dimensional design), can last for up to 25 years and give the designer a monopoly on manufacture of the article. But there are fees to pay and conditions to be met and a registration process to go through and you cannot publish the design or manufacture the article until registration is complete.

An important consideration with design right and registered design is that the commissioner of a design is the first owner of the rights and so the artist loses control of further economic exploitation of the work unless the commissioner agrees to assign the right to the artist. Professional advice will often be needed from a solicitor or patent agent.

Patents

Patents apply to new inventions and are intended to protect the *'function, operation, manufacture or material of construction of an article or an industrial process'.*

Patents give exclusive rights to make use of an invention, and last for a maximum of 20 years. As with registered designs, a patented invention must be new, but may not be an 'artistic creation'. Design protection is only incidental and would only exist where a new invention incorporates a special new design. Help in deciding whether or not a patent is relevant to a design may be obtained from a registered patent agent, or from the Chartered Institute of Patent Agents.

Trade marks

A trade mark identifies one manufacturer's goods to distinguish them from another's. A service mark does the same for services.

Trade marks and service marks may not be directly relevant to artistic production though they can be used to protect character merchandising which is relevant to cartoons. A distinctive word or name can be registered as a trade mark for certain categories of goods and services. Examples are all around us – eg Cadburys, Lego, Harrods. Once registered for a category of product the owner can stop anyone else using the name or mark, or similar names, on the same products.

see 'Cartoons', 3 • Artforms copyright applies to

Artists or craftspeople who wish to develop a trade mark to protect their own works should consult a trade mark or patent agent. A successful registration of a trade mark will take on average two years. There is an application fee of £68 followed by a further fee of £95. The Patent Office publishes a useful pamphlet giving the basic facts on registration, and a more detailed booklet *Registration of Trade Marks or Service Marks*.

The copyright act adds to the Trade Marks Act 1938 the criminal offence of fraudulently using a registered trade mark to try to gain from the use, or at another's expense. For artists who might wish to incorporate trade marks in their work, there is a defence if no gain is intended and there is no attempt to 'pass off' the goods marked with the trade mark as connected with the true user of it. It seems unlikely that an artist would be guilty of an offence by using a trade mark or a shape that was a trade mark.

Passing off

'Passing off' is an attempt to profit from another company's identifiable product by imitating its name or visual appearance and is mainly relevant in the world of commerce.

In a well-documented recent case, a manufacturer who produced hollow plastic lemons to market lemon juice was successfully prosecuted by Colmans, the original makers of 'Jif' plastic lemons. The defendant was guilty of 'passing off' because it was found that there was a risk of consumers being confused into thinking the two products were the same or connected.

Passing off is not likely to be important for most visual artists. It could apply in cases where the work of one artist was very well known to the public, and someone else was producing works which deceived the public into thinking that they were made or authorised by the first artist. So perhaps David Hockney could prevent another artist from issuing prints similar to *A Bigger Splash* which buyers actually thought were Hockney prints. There would only be a case for copyright infringement if there was 'substantial' copying of the original.

Passing off actions can also protect the actual titles of plays, books, performances, etc which are not protected by copyright.

see 16 • Contacts

11 • Transitional provisions

The Copyright Designs and Patents Act 1988 came into force on 1 August 1989, known as the date of commencement. This is the date at which part I, dealing with copyright, began to be applied to all literary, musical, dramatic and artistic works made after 1 August 1989. The other seven shorter parts of the act deal with performance rights (part II), design right (part III & IV), patents and trade marks (part V & VI) and some general provisions (part VII). They have, in some cases, different dates of commencement, or simply amend provisions of older acts.

Before the act came into force there were two relevant rights – copyright and registered design right. There are now four – copyright, unregistered design right, registered design right and moral rights.

The new act is known as the 1988 act because it received the Royal Assent on 15 November 1988. It replaces the previous copyright legislation, covered by the 1956 act. The 1988 UK copyright act is one of the longest of its type in the world and its many provisions apply to the use of copyright material made both before and after the act's commencement. Obviously there is a considerable area of overlap. To cope with works made before the commencement of the new act, we have what are known as 'transitional provisions'.

It is the duration or term of copyright that is most affected by the transitional provisions. Only very gradually will works made after 1 August 1989 begin to predominate in the art market. It is in the nature of the market that artworks are exploited over a long time-span, unlike some other original creative works. This is important to anyone who intends to deal in existing works, whether by copying for publication, or by incorporation in new works.

Some definitions of copyright works have been changed from the 1956 to the 1988 act but work made on or before 1 August 1989 will only have copyright protection after that date if it already had it before that date.

Designs

see 'Use of old designs',
10 • Designs, patents & trade marks

The old copyright law, which protected industrial articles based on drawings of the article will continue to apply for ten years from the 1 August 1989 but with a 'licence of right' during the last five years.

Under the old law, where an artistic work was capable of industrial exploitation and was capable of registration under the Registered Designs Act 1949, the period of copyright protection was limited to fifteen years. This period continues under the new act.

Films

see 'Film',
3 • Artforms copyright applies to

Under the old law the duration of copyright for a film depended on whether the film was registrable or not, and lasted for 50 years from publication or registration. Under the 1988 act copyright lasts for 50 years from release, or 50 years from the making of the film if not released within 50 years. The transitional arrangements depend on whether the film was unpublished on 31 August 1989 – if not then:

• copyright lasts until 31 December 2039, or

• fifty years from publication if published within 50 years.

The new copyright provisions also *'have effect in relation to photographs forming part of a film made before 1 June 1957'*, treating them as photographs, not as single frames in a moving sequence.

Engravings and prints

Copyright in engravings and prints made after 1 August 1989 is now protected for the same length of time as other artistic works, the author's life plus 50 years, instead of 50 years from publication as under the 1956 act. For engravings and prints made before 1 August 1989 the transitional provisions on length of copyright are:

• If published before 1 August 1989 copyright lasts 50 years from publication.

• If unpublished and author dead at 1 August 1989 copyright lasts until 31 December 2039.

• If unpublished but author alive at 1 August 1989 copyright lasts for the author's life plus 50 years.

Photographs

Copyright in photographs made after 1 August 1989 is now protected for the same length of time as other artistic works, the author's life plus 50 years, instead of 50 years from publication as under the 1956 act. For photographs made before 1 August 1989 the transitional provisions on length of copyright are:

• If unpublished at 1 August 1989 copyright lasts until 31 December 2039.
• If published before 1 August 1989 copyright lasts 50 years from publication.

Moral rights

The copyright owner of a work made or commissioned before 1 August 1989 (as defined under the 1956 act) remains the copyright owner. But ownership of moral rights is determined by the provisions of the new act, irrespective of when the work was made. It is theoretically possible for an artist to assert moral rights over a commissioned portrait or photograph made before 1 August 1989 even though, under the provisions of the 1956 act, copyright in that work belongs to the commissioner. However the artist will not be able to object to anything done by or with the consent of the commissioner.

Moral rights as defined in the 1988 act do not apply to any act done before commencement, with one exception. The right to object to false attribution of authorship existed in the 1956 act and so continues to apply. It lasts for the artist's life plus 20 years.

The rights of authorship and integrity do not apply where the author died before 1 August 1989. Where the author had assigned or licensed copyright before 1 August 1989 they cannot exercise moral rights over anything done under the assignment or licence.

Infringements

The new law covering infringement of copyright only applies to acts carried out after commencement. This is important in respect of the new criminal liability for knowingly making or dealing in articles that infringe copyright – the anti-piracy measures.

For acts done before commencement, the provisions of the 1956 continue to apply.

12 • Copyright in other countries

see 'Qualifying persons' 2 • Who owns copyright?

The British copyright act applies to England and Wales, Scotland and Northern Ireland. It applies to work created by UK citizens and to work first published in the UK or other convention countries, and to acts of copying done in the UK. The question of what action can be taken in overseas countries to enforce and protect copyright depends on the law of the country where the work is copied, and where the breach of copyright takes place. In many cases rights are reciprocal between the UK and other countries, so that UK artists will in principle be treated abroad as they would be at home. There are differences, particularly relating to the duration of copyright. In a country where artists' resale right applies, (seven out of twelve European Community (EC) countries have some form of resale right) artists should check to see whether that country's copyright legislation covers non-nationals. The situation in Europe may change in the near future, following EC harmonisation legislation after 1 January 1993.

Berne Convention, Universal Copyright Convention

The copyright act extends protection under UK law, through a statutory instrument to works created by authors from or first published in other so-called 'convention countries'. Similar protection will apply to UK nationals in other convention countries. If copyright protection is more favorable in the other country (eg longer duration then in the UK) convention agreements should give the UK artist that better protection.

The convention countries are those that adhere to international copyright or design right conventions. There are two main international agreements, the Berne Convention and the Universal Copyright Convention (UCC).

Fifty-nine countries worldwide belong to both Berne and UCC, 23 to Berne alone, 22 to UCC alone (mainly third world and USSR). All EC and English speaking countries belong to both Conventions.

One of the main differences between copyright law in the two conventions is the duration of copyright. For Berne countries it is a minimum of the authors life plus fifty years, whereas for UCC countries it is life plus 25 years. Copyright normally needs to be registered in UCC countries and the copyright symbol © is required in these countries as evidence of registration. The symbol should be written with the year of completion, first publication or first performance of the work, and the name of the copyright owner, eg 'AN Artist © 1991'.

The World Intellectual Property Organisation (WIPO) administers the Berne Copyright Convention.

There is also an International Convention for the Protection of Industrial Property. This convention affords certain safeguards in the case of possible exploitation of a design abroad. As a general rule, a design has to be registered separately in each country where it may be exploited, blanket international registration is not possible. 102 countries are declared convention countries for the purposes of design registration. Thirty three countries – mostly members of the Commonwealth – also protect UK registered designs by offering local registration.

Single European Market

The introduction of the Single European Market on 1 January 1993 will include attempts to bring copyright laws into some sort of harmony throughout the EC member countries, though complete harmonisation is unlikely.

The duration of copyright is not yet universal. At present, in Spain it is the author's life plus 60 years; Germany – life plus 70 years; and France – life plus 64 years. In the UK is life plus 50 years. A likely level for harmonisation is life plus 70 years.

Under the Berne Convention moral rights may not be taken away from an author. UK law possibly contravenes this by allowing an artist to waive the moral right of authorship. The British government has signed and ratified Berne, so presumably should be bound by it. The EC has held various consultations and is now reviewing the situation, because of the *considerable differences between Member States on the means of redress (for breach of moral rights) available to the author'.*

The Commission is still undecided as to whether harmonisation for moral rights is needed.

Resale right is an optional provision of the Berne Convention (article 14 ter). Seven of the twelve EC countries operate artists' resale right (also known as droit de suite) in some form. It allows artists to receive a percentage of the profit on second and subsequent resale of their work. The British Government could admit resale right into UK law by an order in council, without the need to amend the copyright act. The official view, however, held by the Office of Arts and Libraries, is that resale right should be regarded as a part of tax legislation if it is used to make contributions to an artists' pension fund – which is what happens in Germany. If this view of resale right is upheld within the EC, then harmonisation is not a matter of majority decision amongst the members of the EC, but a question of individual countries' decisions. If it could be proved that artists and those dealing in art in the UK were seriously disadvantaged by the UK copyright law, because it omits resale right, this might be accepted as a trade barrier or a hindrance to freedom of labour, and against the interests of the Treaty of Rome. The EC Commission proposed in January 1991 to examine resale right *'and the arguments for and against the introduction of such a right'*. A decision on EC action will be taken before 31 December 1992

The International Association of Art (IAA) is lobbying for an EC Charter for the Visual Arts, and has launched a survey of artists' copyright in different European countries. The IAA favours adaption of resale rate thoughout the EEC.

Scandinavia

Some countries, including Norway, have laws that prescribe a form of 'art sales tax' which gives a return to artists, through a central artist-administered fund, in the form of pension and welfare payments. The tax is levied on the income from dealing of all kinds in contemporary art. The British government has argued consistently that this is not a matter for copyright legislation as it is not a matter of artists' rights, but of simple taxation.

Central Europe

Following the breakdown of the centralised, Moscow-controlled Comecon economic union, the countries of central Europe are striving to rebuild their systems of trade and their cultural structures. The institutions of the old Marxist states included artists' collecting societies, copyright laws, and forms of art sales taxes. It is likely that the laws will be reformed along free-market lines, and will be aligned with the EC models. Most central European countries belong to both the Berne and Universal Copyright Conventions.

The most recent (1990) EC copyright proposals for negotiating guidelines on intellectual property rights in a yet wider Europe *'foresee that Poland, Hungary and Czecho-Slovakia will have to agree to join the multilateral agreements'.*

One of the most serious loopholes in copyright protection in eastern and central Europe occurs in the field of computer software. Protection against software theft from western suppliers is often inadequate. Peter Davies of Microsoft, speaking for the industry, said recently *'Either the laws are good on paper but there's no infrastructure to enforce them, or the laws need updating.'*

North America

The USA joined Berne at 1 March 1989, and use of the © symbol is no longer obligatory to register copyright on a work bringing the USA into line with the UK. Title 17, section 401 of the US Copyright Code has been amended accordingly, and should be quoted in case of any difficulty.

In October 1990 the US Congress passed the Visual Artists Rights Act (VRA), which has greatly extended protection of artists' rights. The VRA is expected to come into force in May 1991.

The moral rights covered by the American act are broadly similar to those in the UK. They include attribution of authorship, and the right to have an artist's name removed if a work has been modified in a way not consented to by the artist and which is prejudicial to honour or reputation.

The VRA has established an artist's right to prevent intentional modification, whereas UK moral rights only confer the right to object to such treatment. US artists are also given the right to prevent the destruction of a work, provided it has 'recognized stature'. This is also not possible under the UK act. Although an artist may waive moral rights, it appears that assertion in writing of the right to authorship is not needed in the US.

There are some specific definitions for works qualify for protection under the VRA. A work of visual art is defined as *'a painting, drawing, print, or sculpture, existing in a single copy, in a limited edition of 200 copies or fewer that are signed and consecutively numbered by the author'*. Sculpture and still photographs are similarly limited, to 200 copies or fewer, signed and consecutively numbered.

Canadian copyright law, with its inclusion of Exhibition Payment Right (EPR), allows artists to be paid a royalty on the use of work in certain cases where it is exhibited in public. As with moral rights, EPR cannot be assigned to another person.

Collecting societies

Artists who are members of the Design and Artists Copyright Society will have their rights protected in cert ain other countries through DACS's sister societies abroad.

Licence agreements to use an artist's work will be negotiable through the national rights' society in the country where the work is to be used (ie copied). For example, any organisation originating books, posters, postcards, TV programmes etc in the UK would approach DACS for permission to reproduce a work by a Picasso, whose estate is a member of the French society SPADEM. Similarly a company originating material in Germany would contact the German society. Every society has a standard published tariff of fees.

Copyright and collecting societies worldwide belong to the International Confederation of Societies of Authors and Composers (CISAC) and artists' rights societies belong to the section of CISAC called – International Council of Authors of Graphic and Plastic Art and of Photographers.

Individual artists cannot, practically, and in some cases legally, monitor the use of their copyright work in other countries. The monitoring of foreign exploitation of copyright work can only be satisfactorily handled by a collecting or rights society such as DACS, backed by international organisations.

Convention countries

Countries belonging to both Berne and UCC

Lists based on information in 'A user's guide to copyright', M.F. Flint, Butterworths, 1990

Argentina	Japan
Australia	Lebanon
Austria	Liberia
Bahamas	Liechtenstein
Bangladesh	Luxembourg
Barbados	Malta
Belgium	Mauritius
Brazil	Mexico
Bulgaria	Monaco
Cameroon	Netherlands
Canada	New Zealand
Chile	Norway
Colombia	Pakistan
Costa Rica	Peru
Czecho-Slovakia	Poland
Denmark	Portugal
Fiji	Rwanda
Finland	Senegal
France	South Africa
Germany	Spain
Greece	Sri Lanka
Guinea	Sweden
Holy See	Switzerland
Hungary	Trinidad
Iceland	Tunisia
India	UK
Ireland	USA
Israel	Venezuala
Italy	Yugoslavia

Countries belonging to the Berne Convention only:

Benin	Niger
Central Africa Republic	Phillipines
Chad	Romania
Congo	Singapore
Cyprus	Surinam
Egypt	Thailand
Gabon	Togo
Ivory Coast	Turkey
Libya	Upper Volta
Madegascar	Uruguay
Malaysia	Zaire
Mali	Zimbabwe

Countries belonging to the UCC only

Algeria	Kenya
Andorra	Laos
Belize	Malawi
Cuba	Nicaragua
Dominican Republic	Nigeria
Ecuador	Panama
El Salvador	Paraguay
Ghana	St Vincent
Guatemala	South Korea
Haiti	USSR
Kampuchea (Cambodia)	Zambia

13 • Copyright in brief

What is copyright?

- Copyright protects an artist's exclusive right to reproduce or authorise others to reproduce the artist's work.
- Ownership of copyright in a work is the means by which economic exploitation of a work may be controlled.
- Copyright applies to the 'expression' of an idea not to the idea itself.
- Ownership of copyright in a work is separate to ownership of the work itself.
- Copying of an original work and the issuing of copies to the public is not allowed without the permission of the copyright owner except for a limited number of defined uses (permitted acts) and exceptions.

What does copyright apply to?

- Copyright applies to 'artistic works' (painting, photographs, lithographs, engraving, etching, drawing, collage or sculpture, and works of artistic craftsmanship).
- Works of artistic craftsmanship covers works with an aesthetic rather than purely functional element.

Requirements for copyright protection

- To qualify for copyright protection work must be 'original' in the sense that it must not be a copy.

- Copyright applies only to works existing in a fixed medium. Music, dance or performance must first be annotated on paper or recorded on film or tape before it is covered by copyright protection.
- To fall under the protection of the UK act a work must have been created in the UK; or been created by a 'qualifying person' ie a British citizen, a British Territory Dependent citizen, a British national (overseas), a British Overseas citizen, a British subject or a British Protected Person under the Protected Persons Nationality Act 1981.

Who owns copyright?

- Copyright belongs in the first place to the creator (author) of a work. In the case of work being created as part of the duties of employment (under a 'contract of service') the employer is the first copyright owner not the artist/employee.
- For works made after 1 August 1989 the commissioner of any commissioned artistic work will not own the copyright unless the artist has agreed in writing to transfer it.
- Where two or more artists collaborate in the production of a work, such that their individual contributions are not distinct they have joint authorship in the work and jointly hold the copyright in the work.
- Where two or more artists collaborate on separate elements of a work and their individual contributions are distinct, each artist holds copyright in their own element.
- An artwork can involve separate copyright works with the same or different copyright owners. A photograph of a piece of sculpture, for example, would involve two works and owners – the photographer (if operating in a freelance capacity) owns copyright in the photograph, and the sculptor copyright in the sculpture.

How do you obtain copyright protection?

- Copyright does not need to be recorded or registered in any way – it comes automatically on completion of the work (or in the case of the typographical arrangement of a published edition on the date of first publication).

• The use of the copyright symbol © is not required in the UK and in many other countries but is advisable as it is required in some countries and helps to remind potential users of the existence of copyright and their legal obligations. It should be used with the artist's name and the date of creation (or in the case of the typographical arrangement of a published edition on the date of first publication).

Transferring copyright ownership

• Copyright is not transferred with the sale of the work.
• Ownership of copyright of a work can only be transferred (assigned) to another person or organisation by an agreement in writing signed by the existing copyright owner.
• On death copyright becomes part of the deceased's estate and ownership passes to the artist's heir(s).
• Partial assignments of copyright (ie limited to less than the full period of copyright or to one or more restricted acts) are possible but legal advice will be needed.

Copyright licences

• The copyright owner can licence (give permission) to someone else to copy an artwork. A licence is a contract, either oral or written, defining how the copy/copies of the work may be used and what financial return there is for the copyright owner. A copyright licence does not transfer ownership of copyright.
• A licence may be exclusive, ie the right to reproduce the work is granted exclusively to one person or organisation to the exclusion of the copyright owner, or non-exclusive in which case permission may be given to different people. An exclusive licence must be in writing.
• A licence may be limited – it may grant permission for reproductions to be used only for specified purposes, for a limited period of time and within a specified geographical area.
• A licence may limit the number of reproductions that can be made.

Licence royalties or fees

- Fees and royalties for using reproductions of work vary considerably according to use, the quantities involved and the market strength of the artist
- There are different ways in which payments are made for use of reproductions:
    - flat fee – a single payment suitable for a clearly defined and limited use of the work;
    - repeat fee – for subsequent use of the work; and
    - royalties – a fee based on a percentage of the resale or wholesale price of the product. Regular payments are made on the basis of on the number of sales made in the period. It is common that a percentage of expected royalties is made as a lump sum in advance.

Duration of copyright

- Copyright in an artistic work lasts for the artist's life plus 50 years.
- Copyright in works of joint authorship lasts for the life of the artist living longest plus 50 years.
- Copyright in computer-generated work, film, sound recording and television broadcast or cable transmission lasts for 50 years from the year the work was made.
- Copyright in the typographical arrangement of a published edition lasts for 25 years from publication.
- The length or term of copyright is not affected by assignment.
- The rules differ for works made before 1 August 1989.

Permitted copying

- Limited provision is made within the copyright laws for copying a work without the need to obtain permission from the copyright owner but only for precisely defined purposes – 'the permitted acts' of fair dealing and certain other exceptions. But in the case of fair dealing the copying must be fair, ie the principal motive must not be profit, and the amount of the work being copied must be reasonable.

- The provisions of fair dealing are designed to honour the principle that copyright should not hinder the acquisition of knowledge.
- There are three categories of fair dealing – copying is permitted for:
  - research or private study – single copies only permitted, no acknowledgement necessary (allowing, for example, art students to copy other artworks but not to sell the copy);
  - criticism or review (accompanied by sufficient acknowledgement) – multiple copies are permitted, eg in an issue of a magazine; and
  - the reporting of current events (does not apply to photographs) – multiple copies are permitted, eg in an issue of a newspaper; there must be sufficient acknowledgment except in the case of sound recordings, films or broadcasts.
- Other exceptions include:
  - incidental inclusion in another work; and
  - advertising the sale of an artwork.
- Sculpture and works of artistic craftsmanship permanently sited in public or in premises open to public access may be photographed, filmed, drawn or painted without permission from the copyright owner. Permission must be obtained to copy any works sited in public which are not sculpture or works of artistic craftsmanship;
- For instruction purposes in educational institutions (but the copying must be done by the person giving or receiving instruction and, in the case of artistic works, must not involve a reprographic process, including a photocopier).

Moral rights

- Moral rights protect the artist's and the work's integrity.
- There are four elements to moral rights:
  - the right to be identified as author of a work (the right of authorship or paternity right). This right must be asserted;
  - the right to object to derogatory treatment of the work (integrity right);
  - the right to prevent false attribution of a work to the artist; and
  - the right (of a person commissioning a photograph, film or video for private and domestic purposes) to maintain the privacy of the work that has been made for purely private reasons, eg family events.

- The right of paternity may be asserted in the case of the public exhibition of a work, by ensuring that the artist is identified on the original, or the frame or mount. In other cases it must be asserted in writing in any copyright assignment or other written form, but in these cases not everyone will be bound by the right.
- There are certain exceptions in the act to moral rights.
- Moral rights last for the artist's lifetime plus 50 years (except for the right to prevent false attribution which last for the artist's life plus twenty years).
- Moral rights of the author continue to exist even when copyright has been assigned or licensed, or when the work has been sold.
- Moral rights can not be assigned or licensed to any other person or company.
- Moral rights can be waived in writing – artists should beware of contracts which include a standard clause doing this, such as in commission contracts or terms of entry in open exhibitions.
- Moral rights may also be waived verbally, so always write them into contracts and take steps against any infringements.
- On death moral rights become part of the artist's estate and pass to the artist's heir(s).
- Each author in a work of joint authorship may claim moral rights.

What is copyright infringement?

- An infringement takes place when an unauthorised person commits any of the primary or secondary acts given below, provided there is 'substantial' copying.
- 'Substantial' could refer to the amount copied (even a small percentage could be regarded as substantial), or any essential feature or element.
- Copying does not need to be deliberate to constitute an infringement.
- There are two kinds of infringement:
  - primary infringement – someone illegally copies work, or authorises someone to do illegal copying, and exhibits, publishes or broadcasts it; and

• secondary infringement – someone who knowingly deals commercially in infringing copies (including the provision of premises or apparatus for infringing copies).

What are the remedies for copyright infringement?

• Infringement can be a criminal offence if the person knows or had reason to believe that there was an infringement.
• Civil remedies include:
    • a court injunction to prevent the copying from taking place or continuing; and
    • a court order for the delivery and destruction of infringing copies.
    • compensation for the artist's loss.

How to prevent infringements?

• Ensure proper written contracts are drawn in all dealings with your work clearly defining the copyright position and asserting your moral rights. This includes contracts for commissions, residencies, exhibitions, sales of work, and slide indexes; with agencies; and when commissioning photographs of your work and when releasing them to publishers, etc.
• Consider joining a rights society to 'police' the use of your work for you, and to collect fees on your behalf.

How to deal with an infringer?

• Ask compensation from the infringer.
• Ask for the infringing copies to be handed over to you.
• Seek legal help in pursuing the above or to obtain an injunction preventing further infringement.
• Pursue the claim in the courts if you cannot achieve a voluntary settlement.

Work made before the new act

- Work made before 1 August 1989 is covered by the 1956 copyright act.
- Copyright infringements committed from 1 August 1989 are covered by the 1988 copyright act regardless of when the work was made.
- Moral rights, except the right to false attribution of authorship, do not apply to work made before 1 August 1989.
- Work made before 1 August 1989 has copyright protection after that date only if it had it before that date.
- There are transitional provisions covering the duration of copyright on different types of work made before 1 August 1989.

How does copyright work internationally?

- British copyright law applies to work created in the UK or by 'qualifying persons' (eg British citizens) and to acts of copying done in the UK.
- In other countries the copyright law of that country applies.
- There are two international conventions that try to provide a standardised framework for copyright. Most countries belong to one or the other (or both) the Berne Convention or the Universal Copyright Convention.
- When two convention countries deal with each other the more favourable copyright laws take preference.
- When dealing with non-convention countries (eg China) there will be no reciprocal arrangements unless there is a bilateral copyright agreement between the two countries.

Design right

- The new unregistered design right is automatically owned by the designer except when the design has been commissioned in which case the commissioner is the first owner of design right.
- Design right may be assigned or licensed to others.
- Any original three-dimensional design of any aspect of the shape or configuration of an article is automatically covered by unregistered

Who is the first copyright owner in artistic works?

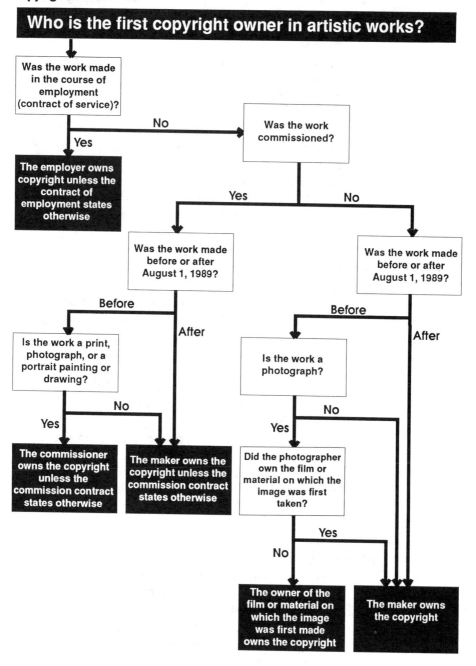

Was the work made in the course of employment (contract of service)?

No → **Was the work commissioned?**

Yes ↓

The employer owns copyright unless the contract of employment states otherwise

From "Was the work commissioned?":

Yes → **Was the work made before or after August 1, 1989?**

No → **Was the work made before or after August 1, 1989?**

From left "before/after" box:

Before → **Is the work a print, photograph, or a portrait painting or drawing?**

After ↓ → **The maker owns the copyright unless the commission contract states otherwise**

From "Is the work a print, photograph, or a portrait painting or drawing?":

Yes → **The commissioner owns the copyright unless the commission contract states otherwise**

No → **The maker owns the copyright unless the commission contract states otherwise**

From right "before/after" box:

Before → **Is the work a photograph?**

After ↓

From "Is the work a photograph?":

Yes → **Did the photographer own the film or material on which the image was first taken?**

No → **The maker owns the copyright**

From "Did the photographer own the film or material on which the image was first taken?":

No → **The owner of the film or material on which the image was first made owns the copyright**

Yes → **The maker owns the copyright**

How long does copyright in artistic works last?

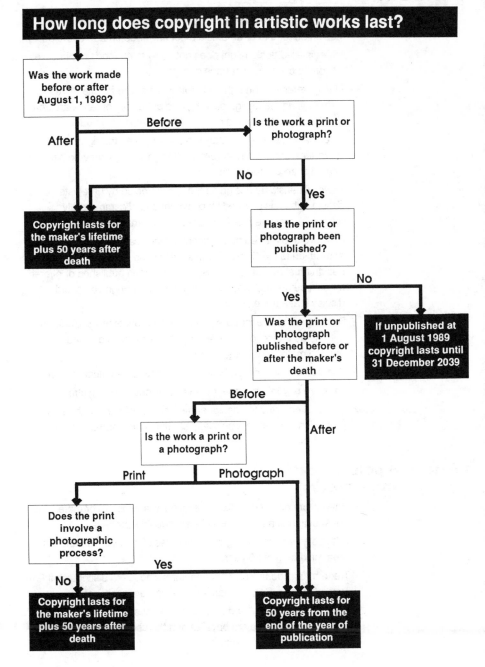

design right. The design must either have been recorded in a design document or an article must have been made to the design.

• Unregistered design right does not apply to methods or principles of construction, or to surface decoration.

• Unregistered design right will protect the article for fifteen years from making the design drawing or a prototype, or ten years from the first marketing of the design, whichever is the shorter.

• Five years after the first marketing anyone has the right to reproduce under licence from the design right owner who can and should charge a fee or royalty.

• A two-dimensional design cannot be protected by unregistered design right. It is covered by copyright and, if commercially exploited, protected for 25 years after first marketing.

• Both two and a three dimensional designs can be registered by application to the Design Registry within the Patent Office. The design must be new and must not have been published or offered for sale before applying for registration – although you could display it at a trade show.

• Designs which are for purely functional products are excluded and there is no protection for features whose shape is dictated by the need to match or for other articles.

• Registered design right affords protection for a maximum of 25 years.

• Fees are payable for registration and extension of registration.

• Registration gives the designer a monopoly of manufacture and protection against 'independent' creation of the same design.

What are patents and trade marks?

• Patents protect the function, operation, manufacture or material of construction of a novel article or an industrial process.

• Patents give exclusive right to make use of an invention and lasts for a maximum of 20 years.

• Trade marks identify one manufacturer's goods to distinguish them from another's. Service marks do the same for services.

• Patents, trade marks and service marks must be registered at the Patents Office. Fees are payable and the use of a registered patent agent can be helpful.

14 • Glossary

The following definitions have been taken from the 'Copyright, Designs and Patents Act 1988'. Textual comments in italics are additions by the editor.

acts restricted by copyright   section 16
(1) The owner of the copyright in a work has... the exclusive right to do the following acts in the UK –
   (a) to copy the work;
   (b) to issue copies of the work to the public;
   (c) to perform, show or play the work in public;
   (d) to broadcast the work or include it in a cable programme service;
   (e) to make an adaptation of the work or do any of the above in relation to an adaptation.

adaptation   section 21
(3) In relation to a literary or dramatic work, means –
   (i) a translation of the work;
   (ii) a version of a dramatic work in which it is converted into a non-dramatic work or, as the case may be, of a non-dramatic work in which it is converted into a dramatic work;
   (iii) a version of the work in which the story or action is conveyed wholly or mainly by means of pictures in a form suitable for reproduction in a book, or in a newspaper, magazine or similar periodical.
(4) In relation to a computer program a 'translation' includes a version of the program in which it is converted into or out of a computer language or code or into a different computer language or code,

otherwise that incidentally in the course of running the program.

artistic work   section 4
(1) ... means –
   (a) a graphic work, photograph, sculpture or collage, irrespective of artistic quality.
   (b) a work of architecture being a building or a model for a building, or
   (c) a work of artistic craftsmanship

assignment (in copyright)   section 90
                    (in design right)   section 222
(1) copyright *(design right)* is transmissible by assignment, by testamentary disposition or by operation of law, as personal or moveable property.
(2) an assignment or other transmission of copyright *(design right)*may be partial, that is, limited so as to apply –
   (a) to one or more, but not all, of the things the copyright *(design right)* owner has the exclusive right to do
   (b) to part, but not the whole, of the period for which the copyright *(design right)* is to subsist.
(3) an assignment of copyright *(design right)* is not effective unless it is in writing signed by or on behalf of the assignor.
Assignment usually means giving copyright (design right) ownership to somebody else.

attribution
(See under 'false attribution', below)

author   section 9
(1) In relation to copyright work means the person who creates it.

blanket licences
Licences issued by a licensing body under a licensing scheme which gives permission to perform certain acts of copying.

broadcast section 6
(1) ... means a transmission by wireless telegraphy of visual images, sounds or other information which –
   (a) is capable of being lawfully received by members of the public, or
   (b) is transmitted for presentation to members of the public.

collecting or rights societies
These are responsible for the collective administration of copyright licensing, royalties and reproduction rights on behalf of individual authors.

collective work section 178
... means –
   (a) a work of joint authorship, or
   (b) a work in which there are distinct contributions by different authors or in which works or parts of works of different authors are incorporated.

(See also 'joint authorship', below)

commercial publication section 175
(2) ... in relation to a literary, dramatic, musical or artistic work means:
   (a) issuing copies of the work to the public at a time when copies made in advance of the receipt of orders are generally available to the public, or
   (b) making the work available to the public by means of an electronic retrieval system.

(See also 'publication', below)

computer-aided work
Computer aided work is work in which the computer has been used in the same way as any other piece of equipment, such as a camera to aid to production.

computer-generated section 178
... in relation to a work, means that the work is generated by a computer in circumstances such that there is no human author of the work.

contract
A contract is an agreement between two or more people. It can be written or verbal.

copy and copying section 17
(2) Copying in relation to a literary, dramatic, musical or artistic work means reproducing the work in any material form. This includes storing the work in any medium by electronic means.
(3) In relation to an artistic work copying includes the making of a copy in three dimensions of a two-dimensional work and the making of a copy in two dimensions of a three-dimensional work.
(4) Copying in relation to a film, television broadcast or cable programme includes making a photograph of the whole or any substantial part of any image forming part of the film, broadcast or cable programme.
(5) Copying in relation to the typographical arrangements of a published edition means making a facsimile copy of the arrangement.
(6) Copying in relation to any description of work includes the making of copies which are transient or are incidental to some other use of the work.

copyright section 1
(1) Copyright is a property right which subsists... in the following descriptions of work –
   (a) original literary, dramatic, musical or artistic works,
   (b) sound recordings, films, broadcasts or cable programmes, and
   (c) the typographical arrangement of published editions.

copyright work section 1
(2) ... means a work of any of those descriptions in which copyright subsists.

(See 'Copyright', above)

Crown copyright section 163
(1) Where a work is made by her Majesty or by an officer or servant of the Crown in the course of his duties –
   (a) the work qualifies for copyright protection notwithstanding... ordinary requirements as to qualification for copyright protection, and

(b) Her Majesty is the first owner of any copyright in the work.

derogatory treatment (in moral rights) section 80
(2) ...
  (a) 'treatment' of a work means any addition to, deletion from or alteration to or adaptation of the work, other than –
    (i) a translation of a literary work or dramatic work, or
    (ii) an arrangement or transcription of a musical work involving no more than a change of key or register; and
  (b) the treatment of a work is derogatory if it amounts to distortion or mutilation of the work or is otherwise prejudicial to the honour or reputation of the author or director.

design (in design right) section 213
(2) ... means the design of any aspect of the shape or configuration (whether internal or external) of the whole or part of an article
(4) A design is not 'original' for the purposes (of this part of the Act) if it is commonplace in the design field in question at the time of its creation.

A design must deal with the shape or configuration of an article and must be original.

design document (in design right) section 263
... means any record of a design, whether in the form of a drawing, a written description, a photograph, data stored in a computer or otherwise.

design right section 213
(1) ... is a property right which subsists... in an original design
(3) Design right does not subsist in –
  (a) a method or principle of construction
  (b) features of shape or configuration of an article which –
    (i) enable the article to be connected to, or placed in, around or against another article so that either article may perform its function, or
    (ii) are dependent upon the appearance of another article of which the article is intended by the designer to form an integral part, or

(c) surface decoration.

design right (owner of) section 226
(1) ... the owner of design right in a design has the exclusive right to reproduce the design for commercial purposes –
  (a) by making articles to that design, or
  (b) by making a design document recording the design for the purpose of enabling such articles to be made.

A design may be exploited for commercial purposes by the owner of the design right.

designer (in design right) section 214
(1) ... in relation to a design, the person who creates it.

designer of computer-generated design (in design right) section 214
(2) ... the person by whom the arrangements necessary for the creation of the design are undertaken shall be taken to be the designer.

dramatic work section 3
(1) ... includes a work of dance or mime.

employed, employee section 178
... employment under a contract of service or of apprenticeship.

exclusive licence section 92
(1) ... means a licence in writing signed by or on behalf of the copyright (or design right) owner authorising the licensee to the exclusion of all other persons, including the person granting the licence, to exercise a right which would otherwise be exercisable exclusively by the copyright (or design right) owner.

An exclusive licence grants the reproduction rights to one person or organisation and thus excludes all other people (including the person granting the licence) from copying the work.

facsimile section 178
... includes a copy which is reproduced or enlarged in scale

false attribution (in moral rights) section 84
(1) A person has the right... –
  (a) not to have a literary, dramatic, musical

or artistic work falsely attributed to him as author, and

(b) not to have a film falsely attributed to him as a director;

and in this section an 'attribution', in relation to such a work, means a statement (express or implied) as to who is the author or director.

film   **section 5**

... a recording on any medium from which a moving image may by any means be produced.

first ownership (of copyright)

First ownership of copyright belongs to the author of the work, unless they are employed to produce the work or it is crown or parliamentary copyright.

future copyright   **section 91**

(2) Copyright which will or may come into existence in respect of a future work or class of works or on the occurrence of a future event.

Copyright can be assigned or licensed for works yet to be created.

graphic work   **section 4**

(2) ... includes –
   (a) any painting, drawing, diagram, map, chart or plan, and
   (b) any engraving, etching, lithograph, woodcut or similar work.

infringements (in design right)   section 226

(3) Design right is infringed by a person who without the license of the design right owner does, or authorises another to do, anything which... is the exclusive right of the design right owner.

infringements (in copyright)   section 16

(2) Copyright in a work is infringed by a person who, without the licence of the copyright owner does, or authorises another to do, any of the act restricted by the copyright.

(See also 'acts restricted by copyright', above)

joint authorship   **section 10**

(1) ... means a work produced by the collaboration of two or more authors in which the contribution of each author is not distinct from that of the other author or authors.

joint design (in design right)   section 259

(1) ... means a design produced by the collaboration of two or more designers in which the contribution of each is not distinct from that of the other or others.

licences

A copyright licence is a contract, either oral or written, giving permission for someone to copy a work under copyright.

literary work   **section 3**

(1) ... means any work, other than a dramatic or musical work, which is written, spoken or sung, and accordingly includes –
   (a) a table or compilation, and
   (b) a computer program.
(See also 'computer-generated work', above)

made (recorded)   **section 3**

(2) Copyright does not subsist in a literary, dramatic or musical work unless and until it is recorded, in writing or otherwise; and references... to the time at which such a work is made are to the time at which it is so recorded.

(3) It is immaterial for the purposes of subsection (2) whether the work is recorded by or with the permission of the author; and where it is not recorded by the author, nothing in that subsection affects the question whether the copyright subsists in the record as distinct from the work recorded.

Ownership of copyright comes when the work is made, recorded or fixed in a stable medium. It does not matter if this occurs without the permission of the author.

making articles to a design (in design right)   section 226

(1) ... reproduction of a design by making articles to the design means copying the design so as to produce articles exactly or substantially to that design.

moral rights

The new statutory moral rights introduced by the 1988 act.

musical work   **section 3**

(1) ... means a work consisting of music,

exclusive of any words or action intended to be sung, spoken or performed with the music.

non-exclusive licence

In relation to copyright a licence which gives some limited rights but not the exclusive right which would otherwise be exercisable exclusively by the copyright owner. (See 'exclusive licence' and 'blanket licence', above)

Parliamentary copyright   section 165
(1) ... where a work is made by or under the direction or control of the House of Commons or House of Lords –
 (a) the work qualifies for copyright protection notwithstanding... ordinary requirements as to qualification for copyright protection, and
 (b) the House by whom, or under whose direction or control, the work is made is the first owner of any copyright in the work, and if the work is made by or under the directionor control of both Houses, the two Houses are joint first owners of copyright
(4) ... works made *(as described in (1) above)* include –
 (a) any work made by an officer or employee of the House in the course of his duties, and
 (b) any sound recording, film, live broadcast or live cable programme of the proceedings of that House.

First ownership of the Parliamentary copyright belongs to the House under whose direction ithe work was made.

patents

Patents give exclusive rights to make use of an invention and last for 20 years.

paternity right
(See 'Right of authorship', below)

performance (in copyright)   section 19
(1) The performance of the work in public is an act restricted by the copyright in a literary, dramatic, or musical work.
(2) ... performance, in relation to a work –
 (a) includes delivery in the case of lectures, addresses, speeches and sermons, and

(b) in general, includes any mode of visual or acoustic presentation, including presentation by means of a sound recording, film, broadcast or cable programme of the work.
(3) The playing or showing of the work in public is an act restricted by the copyright in a sound recording, film, broadcast or cable programme.

Performance (in rights in performances)
                                                 section 180
(2) ... means –
 (a) dramatic performance (which includes dance and mime),
 (b) a musical performance,
 (c) a reading or recitation of a literary work, or
 (d) a performance of a variety act or any similar presentation,
which is, or so far as it is, a live performance given by one or more individuals; and 'recording', in relation to a performance, means a film or sound recording –
 (a) made directly from the live performance,
 (b) made from a broadcast of, or cable programme including, the performance, or
 (c) made, directly or indirectly, from another recording of the performance.

Under the 'rights in performance' section a performance is defined as a dramatic performance, musical performance, a reading or recitation of a literary work or the performance of a variety act.

primary infringement
Primary infringement occurs when someone illegally copies work, or authorises someone to do illegal copying, and exhibits, publishes or broadcasts it.

publication   section 175
(1) ... in relation to a work –
 (a) means the issue of copies to the public, and
 (b) includes, in the case of a literary, dramatic, musical or artistic work, making it available to the public by means of an electronic retrieval system.
(4) The following do not constitute publication...
 (b) in the case of an artistic work –
  (i) the exhibition of the work,

(ii)   the issue to the public of copies of a graphic work representing, or of photographs of, a work of architecture in the form of a building or a model for a building, a sculpture or a work of artistic craftsmanship,

(iii) the issue to the public of copies of a film including the work, or

(iv)   the broadcasting of the work or its inclusion in a cable programme service (otherwise than for the purpose of an electronic retrieval system).

(See also 'commercial publication', above)

recording rights (in rights in performances) section 185

(1)   ... an 'exclusive recording contract' means a contract between a performer and another person under which that person is entitled to the exclusion of all other persons (including the performer) to make recordings of one or more of his performances with a view to their commercial exploitation.

An exclusive recording right gives the recording rights to one person in to the exclusion of all the others, including the person giving the rights and the performer.

reprographic process, copy, & copying section 178

... means a process –

(a)   for making facsimile copies, or

(b)   involving the use of an appliance for making multiple copies, and includes, in relation to a work held in electronic form, any copying by electronic means, but does not include the making of a film or sound recording.

restricted acts

(See under 'acts restricted by copyright', above)

right of authorship (in moral rights) section 44

(4)   The author of an artistic work has the right to be identified whenever –

(a)   the work is published commercially or exhibited in public, or a visual image of it is broadcast or included in a cable programme service;

(b)   a film including a visual image of the work is shown in public or copies of such a film are issued to the public; or

(c)   in the case of a work of architecture in the form of a building or model of a building, a sculpture or a work of artistic craftsmanship, copies of a graphic work representing it, or of a photograph of it, are issued to the public.

right of integrity (in moral rights) section 80

(4)   In the case of an artistic work the right is infringed by a person who –

(a)   publishes commercially or exhibits in public a derogatory treatment of the work, or broadcasts or includes in a cable programme service a visual image of a derogatory treatment of the work,

(b)   shows in public a film including a visual image of a derogatory treatment of the work or issues to the public copies of such a film, or

(c)   in the case of –

(i)   a work of architecture in the form of a model for a building,

(ii)   a sculpture, or

(iii) a work of artistic craftsmanship, issues to the public copies of a graphic work representing, or of a photograph of, a derogatory treatment of the work.

sculpture section 4

(2)   ... includes a cast or model made for purposes of sculpture.

secondary infringment

Secondary infringment occurs when someone knowingly deals commercially in illegal copies but does not actually do or authorise the copying themselves.

service marks

A service mark identifies one manufacturer's service to distinguish it from another's.

sound recording section 5

(1)   ... means –

(a)   a recording of sounds, from which the sounds may be reproduced, or

(b)   a recording of the whole or any part of a literary, dramatic or musical work, from which sounds reproducing the work or part may be produced, regardless of the medium on which the recording is made or the method by which the sounds are reproduced or produced.

sufficient acknowledgement section 178
... means an acknowledgement identifying the work in question by its title or other description, and identifying the author.

sufficient disclaimer section 178
... in relation to an act capable of infringing the right conferred by section 80 (right to object to derogatory treatment of work), means a clear and reasonably prominent indication (that the work has been subjected to treatment to which the author or director has not consented) –
  (i) given at the time of the act, and
  (ii) if the author or director is then identified, appearing along with the identification.

trade marks
A trade mark identifies one manufacturer's goods to distinguish them from another's.

transitional provisions
Transitional provisions deal with the overlap between the introduction of the 1988 copyright act and the previous 1956 act.

unauthorised section 178
... as regards anything done in relation to a work, means done otherwise than –
  (a) by or with the licence of the copyright owner, or
  (b) if copyright does not subsist in the work, by or with the licence of the author or, in a case where section 11(2) *(work made by an employee)* would have applied, the author's employer or, in either case, persons lawfully claiming under him, or
  (c) in pursuance of section 48 (copying etc of certain material by the Crown)

Anything that is done other than under the licence or permission of the copyright owner is an unauthorised act. (See also 'employed', above)

unknown authorship section 9
(5) ... the identity of an author shall be regarded as unknown if it is not possible for a person to ascertain his identity by reasonable inquiry; but if his identity is once known it shall not subsequently be regarded as unknown.

Copyright exists even when the author of a work is unknown.

writing section 178
... includes any form of notation or code, whether by hand or otherwise and regardless of the method by which, or medium in or on which, it is recorded, and 'written' shall be construed accordingly.

Any form of notation or code in any medium is considered writing under the terms of the act.

15 • Further reading

Visual art publications covering copyright

Art Monthly 'Artlaw' column. A regular feature in *Art Monthly* which has covered copyright. Contact *Art Monthly*, 36 Great Russell Street, London, WC1B 3PP 071 580 4168

'Help' page questions in Artists Newsletter. Collected questions and answers on copyright from the 'Help' pages of *Artists Newsletter*. £1.50 from AN Publications, PO Box 23 Sunderland, SR4 6DG

Making Ways: the visual artists guide to surviving and thriving. D Butler (ed), AN Publications, 1989, ISBN 0 907 730 043. *(A complete guide to the skills needed to succeed as a self-employed artist including a chapter on copyright – available by mail order from AN Publications, PO Box 23, Sunderland, SR4 6DG at £11.95)*

Photographers guide to the Copyright Act, 1988. British Photographer's Liaison Committee, 1989, ISBN 0 951 467 107. 9-10 Domingo Street, London EC1A 0TA

Rights: The Illustrators guide to professional practice. S Stern (ed) The Associations of Illustrators, 1989, ISBN 0 951 544 802. 1 Colville Place, off Charlotte Street, London W1P 1HN

Writers and Artists Year Book 1991. A & C Black, 1991, ISBN 0 713 632 798

Copyright

A users guide to copyright. M F Flint, Butterworths, 1990, ISBN 0 406 200 750

Blackstone's Guide to the Copyright, Designs and Patents Act 1988. G Dworkin and R D Taylor, Blackstone Press Ltd, 1989, ISBN 1 854 310 232. *(Includes a copy of the Act)*

Copyright, basic facts. The Patent Office, 1990, DTI/Pub 232/30K/2/90

Copyright: A practical guide. W S Strong, MIT, 1990, ISBN 0 262 192 926

Copyright clearance: A practical guide. G Crabb, National Council for Educational Technology, 1990, ISBN 0 861 841 913

Copyright, Designs and Patents Act 1988. HMSO, 1988, ISBN 0 105 448 885

Copyright: Interpreting the Law for Libraries and Archives. G P Cornish, Library Association, 1990, ISBN 0 853 657 092

Intellectual property, patents, copyright, trade marks and allied rights. W R Cornish, Sweet & Maxwell, 1989, ISBN 0 421 379 707

Law of copyright and rights in performances. D De Freitas, British Copyright Council, 1990, ISBN 0 901 737 054

Photocopying from books and journals: A guide for all users of copyright literay works. C Clark (ed), British Copyright Council, 1990, ISBN 0 901 737 062

Understanding copyright: A practical guide. E A Thorn, Jay Books, 1989, ISBN 1 870 404 033

What is intellectual property? The Patent Office, 1990, DTI/Pub 233/30K/2/90

Design Right

Books and leaflets published by from The Patent Office can be obtained The Patents Office, Designs Registry, Cardiff Road, Newport, Gwent, NP1 1RH 0633 814 000.

Applying to register a design (temporary revision August 1989). The Patent Office, 1989

Introducing design registration (temporary edition August 1989). The Patent Office, 1989

Law of industrial design: registered designs, copyright and design right. C Tootall, CCH Editions, 1989, ISBN 0 863 252 230

Registered designs, basic facts. The Patent Office, 1990, DTI/Pub 230/30K/2/90

16 • Contacts

Organisations involved with copyright and related rights

Authors' Licensing and Collecting Society Ltd (ALCS), 33-34 Alfred Place, London WC1E 7DP tel 071 255 2034. The ALCS deals primarily with the rights of authors, but as Public Lending Right (PLR) and Reprography Right in published work also cover the work of illustrators, the Society will be relevant to some artists.

British Copyright Council (BCC), 29-33 Berners Street London W1P 4AA tel 071 359 1895. An umbrella organisation that co-ordinates lobbying and consultation for all copyright owners, including artists. Members of the BCC include the: Association of Illustrators, British Actors' Equity, British Institutue of Professional Photography, Chartered Society of Designers, Design & Artists Copyright Society, National Union of Journalists, Royal Academy of Arts, Royal Photographic Society.

British Library, Science Reference & Information Service, 25 Southampton Buildings, London WC2A 1AW tel 071 323 7494. This is the address for all general enquires concerning design right in the UK and for information about patents, trademark and design right abroad. For specific enquiries about Design Registration contact the Patent Office.

British Photographic Industry Copyright Association, Roxburghe House, 273 287 Regent Street, London W1R 7BP. Deals with copyright issues across the photographic industry.

British Photographers' Liaison Committee, 9-10 Domingo Street, London EC1 0TA tel 071 608 1441. Involved in the development of the 1988 act, the committee can provide advice and information.

Chartered Institute of Patent Agents, Staple Inn Buildings, London WC1V 7PZ tel 071 405 9450. The institute can provide details of agents who are licensed to negotiate the registration of patents.

Copyright Licensing Agency Ltd (CLA), 90 Tottenham Court Road, London W1P 9HE tel 071 436 5931. At present the CLA only covers copying in paper form of books, learned journals and periodicals but efforts are being made by the CLA to deal with the copying of artistic works. It is also responsible for licensing educational establishments for certain permitted use of copyright material.

Copyright Registry, Stationers' Hall, Ludgate Hill, London EC4M 7DD. Although registration of copyright is not legally necessary, the Copyright Registry exists to provide a safety net for anyone who wishes to have their copyright ownership recorded.

Design & Artists Copyright Society Ltd (DACS), St. Mary's Clergy House, 2 Whitechurch Lane, London E1 7QR tel 071 247 1650. The Society for all visual artists including photographers, and art video-makers. DACS looks after members' copyright interests, checking on infringements and collecting reproduction fees. At the end of 1990 DACS had signed agreements with 23 societies representing members' interests worldwide. Links through CIAGP, a par of CISAC , provide reciprocal services for artists and other copyright owners whose works are exploited outside the country in which they were made.

Educational Recording Agency, 14 Hanover Square, London W1R 7QR. Covers visual art through the involvement of DACS.

International Confederation of Societies of Authors & Composers (CISAC), 11 Rue Keppler, F - 75116, Paris, France. There is a specialist artists section, the International Council of Authors of Graphic & Plastic Art and Photographers (CIAGP) – see below.

International Council of Authors of Graphic & Plastic Art and Photographers (CIAGP), 11 Rue Keppler, F - 75116, Paris, France. Each country worldwide has one officially recognised artists' rights society. This international network of societies ensures that works of art made in the UK receive reciprocal treatment abroad, and vice versa.

Mechanical Copyright Protection Society Ltd (MCPS), Elgar House, 41 Streatham High Road, London SW16 1ER tel 081 769 4400. Is responsible for issuing licences for the recording of music and the issuing of copies to the public – ie disks, tapes, etc. The MCPS acts on behalf of composers and music publishers in collecting royalties. See also PRS and PPL.

Patent Office, Designs Registry, Cardiff Rd, Newport, Gwent NP1 1RH tel 0633 814000. The Patent Office houses the Register of Designs and deals with applications for Design Right registration. Application to inspect existing registered designs should also be made to the Patent Office.

Performing Right Society Ltd (PRS), 29-33 Berners Street, London W1P 4AA tel 071 580 5544. A collecting society for composers, performers and other owners of copyright in music. It exists to license premises and collect fees for the performance of music of all kinds.

Phonographic Performance Ltd (PPL), Ganton House, 14 Ganton Street, London W1V 1LB tel 071 437 0311. Licences are issued to control the public playing and broadcast of records. The licensing of premises for the public playing of music is a legal obligation, and is an important channel by which musicians and composers share in the economic exploitation of their work.

Public Lending Right Office (PLR), Bayheath House, Prince Regent Street, Stockton-on-Tees, Cleveland TS18 1DF. Authors (including artists who produce books) may receive payment in respect of borrowings of their works from public libraries.

Public Record Office, Ruskin Avenue, Kew, Richmond, Surrey TW9 4DU (071) 876 3444. Information about the existence & identity of authors of works, eg whether or not the work is still in copyright, may be obtained from the Public Record Office.

The Society of Authors, 84 Drayton Place, London SW10 9FB tel 071 373 6642. International organisation for collecting and rights societies that are responsible for the collective administration of copyright licensing, royalty and reproduction rights, on behalf of individual authors.

Video Performance Ltd (VPL), Ganton House, 14-22 Ganton Street, London W1V 1LB tel 071 437 0311. Deals with the regulation of use and exploitation of video recordings.

Professional organisations

These may be able to help with problems and queries about copyright in particular artforms or industries.

Association of Artists in Ireland (AAI), Room 803, Liberty Hall, Dublin 1, Ireland tel 010 3531 740529

Association of Illustrators (AOI), 1 Colville Place, London W1P 1HN tel 071 636 4100

Association of Photographers (AFAE), 9-10 Domingo Street, London EC1Y 0TA tel 071 608 1441

British Actors' Equity Association, 8 Harley Street, London W1N 2AB tel 071 636 6367. As performance or live art falls within performance rights, part II of the copyright Act, this is the best trade union to go to for collective protection of these rights.

British National Committee of the International Artists Association, c/o 49 Stainton Road, Sheffield S11 7AX tel 0742 669889. The committee is an umbrella organisation, run by representatives of artists' associations in England, Scotland, & Wales. Its primary concern is with the status of professional artists, with a strong emphasis on artists' rights including copyright.

Chartered Society of Designers, 29 Bedford Square, London WC1 tel 071 631 1510

Composers' Guild of Great Britain, 34 Hanway Street, London W1P 9DE tel 071 436 0007

Federation of British Artists (FBA), 17 Carlton House Terrace, London SW1 tel 071 930 6844. The FBA is the umberella organisation for a number of artists' societies including the Royal Society of British Artists and the Royal Society of Portrait Painters. In 1989 it organised 2 seminars on the 1988 copyright Act and papers from the seminars may still be available.

International Association of Art (IAA/AIAP), 1, rue Miollis 75732 Paris, CEDEX 15 France tel 010 33 1 45 66 57 57. There is a network of national committees of the IAA throughout the world, providing information on artists' rights, and other professional concerns. Britain and Ireland are represented by the Irish National Committee, c/o the Association of Artists in Ireland (AAI) and the British National Committee of the IAA.

Music Publishers Association, 7th Floor, Kingsway House, 103 Kingsway, London WC2B 6QX tel 071 831 7591

Musicians' Union, 60-62, Clapham Road, London SW9 0JJ tel 071 582 5566

National Artists Association (NAA), Membership Secretary, 17 Shakespeare Terrace, Sunderland SR2 7JG. The national organisation for artists and craftsworkers, offers advice, codes of practice, specimen contracts, etc. Membership of the NAA includes a reduced rate membership of DACS. The NAA is involved with setting up professional qualifications for artists, and with the protection of artists rights in collaboration with other organisations.

Printmakers' Council, 31 Clerkenwell Close, London EC1 tel 071 250 1927

Producers' Association, Paramount House, 162/170 Wardour Street, London W1V 4LA tel 071 434 0181. The professional association for film producers.

Publishers' Association, 19 Bedford Square, London WC1 tel 071 580 6321. The association deals with all matters affecting the copyright status of published works.

Publishers Licensing Society, 33 -34 Alfred Place, London WC1E 7DP tel 071 436 5931. The society aims to protect and enforce publishers' rights in copyright.

Index

Index • 17

Fax 28
Fees 58; advances 60; flat fees 58; negotiating rates 61; repeat fees 59; royalties 59
Films 29; ownership of copyright 12; transitional provisions 89
First ownership of copyright 12
Fixation of work 10
Flat fees 58
Folk art 29
Future copyright 51

G

Galleries 71; exception to copyright 44; photographing work 71
Glass 30
Graphic design 30
Graphic work 10, 27

H

Holography 10, 37

I

Idea-expression dichotomy 8
Illustration 30
Inclusion in other works 70
Industrial designs 80; length of copyright 80
Infringements of copyright 62; primary infringement 62; secondary infringement 62; transitional provisions 90
Installation 31

J

Joint authorship 15; community art 24

L

Legal advice 64
Length of copyright 17, 80; crown copyright 14; industrial designs 80; parliamentary copyright 14
Length of design right 81; registered design right 84;
Length of patents 86
Libraries 48
Licences 51; blanket 55; exclusive 51; non-exclusive 51, 53
Licensing copyright 17
Licensing design right 81
Licensing schemes 55
Literary works 20
Live art. See Performance art

M

Mail art 32
Monitoring copyright 19
Moral rights 7, 73; assertion of 75; computer art 26; contracts 54; employment 14, 75; exceptions to 76, 77; exhibitions 43; infringements of 64; length of 76; open competitions 79; ownership of 12; photography 37; public art 38; public display of work 46; reporting 76, 77; right of authorship 75, 79; right of integrity 76, 79; right of privacy 78; right of refuting

authorship 78; right to prevent false attribution 79; transfer of 51, 78; transitional provisions 90; waiver of 79
Multiples. See Sculpture
Murals 32, 48

N

Non-exclusive licence 51, 53
News reporting. See Reporting

O

Open competitions 57; moral rights 79
Originality 11; design right 81
Ownership of copyright 12; commissions 13; employment 13; first ownership 12; transfer of 17

P

Painting 33
Parliamentary copyright 14
Parody 33
Partial assignments 17, 55
Passing off 86
Patents 85
Performance art 34
Performance rights 35; sound recordings 40
Permitted acts 67. See also Fair dealing; copying 72; copying in educational establishments 69; inclusion in other work 70; libraries 48; public display of work 71; sculpture 71; works of artistic craftsmanship 71
Photo agencies 49
Photo libraries 49
Photocopying 35; educational establishments 69
Photography 10, 36; moral rights 37; transitional provisions 90
Picture loan schemes 50
Placements 14, 46
Portraiture 33, 37
Postcards 45
Posters 45, 72
Primary infringements 62
Printmaking 38; transitional provisions 89
Private study 67
Proving ownership 16
Pseudonymous authorship 16, 71
Public art 38, 45, 46; design right 45; moral rights 38; works of artistic craftsmanship 45
Public display of work 38; moral rights 46; permitted acts 71
Public domain 17
Published works: term of copyright 20
Publishing work 13

Q

Qualifying persons 13

R

Rates of pay. See Fees
Registered design right 85; exceptions 83; length of 84

124

If you have found this book useful...

you will want to know more about AN Publications. We are the only publishers to specialise in information for visual artists, photographers, time-based artists and craftspeople. So if you need to know:

what awards, competitions are in the offing
which galleries are worth approaching to show your work
how to make the most of your skills
who supplies the materials you need at the best prices
where to find help, information and advice
when to apply for grants

and any other practical information, we can help you through our directories, handbooks, 'Fact Packs' and monthly magazine, *Artists Newsletter*. See order form

Artists Newsletter	The essential monthly magazine packed with up-to-the-minute information on residencies, awards, commissions, jobs, competitions, etc
Making Ways (2nd edition)	The only handbook written by artists for artists, with first-hand advice on all aspects of surviving and thriving as a visual artist or maker Ed David Butler. 368 pages A5
Directory of Exhibition Spaces (2nd edition)	A comprehensive listing of over 2000 exhibition spaces in the UK and Eire which helps you find the ideal exhibition space for your work. Gives details of application procedure, policy and exhibition space. Ed Susan Jones. 500 pages A5
HANDBOOKS	A series of source books for artists, craftspeople and photographers
Artists Handbooks 1	**Residencies in Education:** *setting them up and making them work* Explores the strengths and weaknesses of 6 residencies, to help you get the best out of placements of all kinds. By Daniel Dahl, ed Susan Jones, commissioned by Yorkshire Arts. 124 pages A5
Artists Handbooks 2	**Health & Safety:** *making art & avoiding dangers* Making art can be dangerous. Artists and makers now use substances and processes which could damage human health and the environment. By Tim Challis and Gary Roberts. 128 pages A5
Artists Handbooks 3	**Money Matters:** *the artist's financial guide* Professional help on disentangling your finances. Accountants experienced in the particular problems of artists offer user-friendly advice on: tax, national insurance, VAT; keeping accounts; pricing your work; grants; insurance; dealing with customers; suppliers and banks; and much more. Features an accounting system specially devised for visual artists. By Sarah Deeks, Richard Murphy & Sally Nolan. 128 pages A5
Artists Handbooks 5	**Organising Your Exhibition: the self-help guide** By Debbie Duffin. 128 pages A5

FACT PACKS	A series of factsheets which form an invaluable information resource.
Fact Pack 1	**Rates of Pay** by Susan Jones. Detailed information on current pay rates for artists. Looks at different sectors and parts of the country.
Fact Pack 2	**Slide Indexes** by Susan Jones. A review of slide indexes, their effectiveness and which artforms fare best. Includes a national listing of artists' registers and slide indexes
Fact Pack 3	**Mailing the Press** by David Butler & Caroline Lambert, it includes a press list of national dailies, weeklies, magazines, TV and radio stations.
Fact Pack 4	**Getting TV & Radio Coverage** by Paul Gough & Caroline Lambert, help from an arts programme presenter on TV South West and Head of Painting at Bristol Polytechnic. Includes a contact list of TV and radio stations. Advice on writing a press release and sending photographs to the press.
Fact Pack 5	**Craft Fairs** by Kathryn Salomon, how to identify the right fairs for you. How to apply. And how to make the most of them. Includes a selected list fo national and international fairs with details.
Fact Pack 6	**Insurance** by Chris McCready, a guide to insurance for artists, specially commissioned by AN Publications. Advises on types of insurance artists need, and why.
Basic Survival Facts	By Artists Newsletter staff, essential practical information for all new artists on getting started. Tackles money, opportunities, exhibiting, selling, studios and who to contact for what.
PHOTOGRAPHY	Two essential books for all those working in independent photography
Independent Photography Directory	Ed Mike Hallett & Barry Lane. Published for the Arts Council. Listing of over 250 organisations involved with photography plus invaluable infomation on awards, fellowships, professional organisations, funding bodies, press lists, etc. 224 pages, A5
Code of Practice for Independent Photography	Guidelines for successful negotiations with advice on employment, copyright, exhibiting, commissions... plus sample fees and rates of pay. For anyone who exhibits, buys or sells, or commissions any visual art work. Ed Vince Wade. 32 pages A5
OTHER BOOKS	We also supply (mail order only) books produced by other publishers aimed at the practising artist and arts administration, please ask for our brochure.

AN Publications, PO Box 23, Sunderland SR4 6DG. Tel 091 567 3589. Fax 091 564 1600

346. 0482/M12

ORDER FORM

	Qty	£
Only UK prices given, phone for overseas prices		
Artists Handbooks 1: Residencies in Education £7.25		
Artists Handbooks 2: Health & Safety £7.25		
Artists Handbooks 3: Money Matters £7.25		
Artists Handbooks 5: Organising Your Exhibition £7.25		
Directory of Exhibition Spaces £12.50		
Making Ways £11.99		
Independent Photography Directory £5.00		
A Code of Practice for Photography £3.25		
Artists Newsletter £15.00 UK individual, £25.00 UK institution Annual subscription beginning with _____ issue		
Fact Pack Subscription (6 Fact Packs) beginning with issue number _____ UK £8.50		
Fact Pack 1: Rates of Pay £1.50		
Fact Pack 2: Slide Indexes £1.50		
Fact Pack 3: Mailing the Press £1.50		
Fact Pack 4: Getting TV & Radio Coverage £1.50		
Fact Pack 5 : Craft Fairs £1.50		
Fact Pack 6: Insurance £1.50		
Basic Survival Facts £1.50		
	TOTAL	

Please pay all overseas orders in £ Sterling

Name/Address

Name

Address

Postcode   Telephone

Payment by cheque/postal

Send cheque/postal order made payable to AN Publications

Return to: AN Publications, FREEPOST, PO Box 23, Sunderland SR1 1BR

Payment by credit card   NB Visa/MasterCard only

Card number

Expiry date

Return to: AN Publications, FREEPOST, PO Box 23, Sunderland SR1 1BR

Telephone orders 091 514 3600 (Mon – Fri 9-5)

I obtained this form from:

Valid until 31/7/91